Teachers' Prayers of Blessing, Liturgy, and Lament

This Year, Lord

Sheila Quinn Delony

This Year, Lord

Teachers' Prayers of Blessing, Liturgy, and Lament

Copyright @ 2021 by Sheila Quinn Delony

All rights reserved. Written permission must be secured from the publisher to use or reproduce any part of this book, except for brief quotations in critical reviews or articles.

Requests for permission can be addressed to
sheilaquinnresources@gmail.com.

ISBN: 978-0-578-98247-2

Printed in the United States of America.

Interior design by Left Coast Design, Bruce Deroos.

Dedication

For the teachers

Contents

Introduction	15
Introduction to Liturgies for Common Work	21
LITURGIES FOR COMMON WORK	**23**
For Another Day	23
Sunday	23
Monday	24
Tuesday	24
Wednesday	24
Thursday	24
Friday	24
Saturday	25
Greeting Students before Class	25
Lunch Count	25
Morning Meeting	26
Taking Attendance	26
Pacing	26
Before Teaching a Math Lesson	27
Before Teaching a Language Arts Lesson	27
Before Teaching a Science Lesson	28
Before Teaching a Social Studies Lesson	28
Lunch	29
Recess	29
Coming in from Recess	29
Reading Aloud	30
Guided Reading	30
Stations	30
Laminating Materials	31
Making Copies	31

Contents

Giving Children Internet Access	32
Instructional Technology	32
Redirecting a Student	33
Library Day	33
Packing Up at the End of the Day	34
As My Students Leave	34
After the Students Are Gone	34
Tutoring	34
Faculty Meetings	35
Before Reading Emails	35
IEP Meetings	36
Virtual Meetings	36
On Social Media	37
Virtual Class	37
Before Calling a Parent	38
Lesson Planning	38
Grading Papers	39
Displaying Student Work	39
Time Management	39
Boundaries for My Time	40
Sense of Humor	40
Introduction to the Blessings for Seasons	43
BLESSINGS FOR SEASONS	**45**
Setting Up a Classroom	45
Meet the Teacher Night	46
Beginning of a School Year	46
Parent-Teacher Conferences	48
The Longest Stretch	48
Picture Day	50
Assembly	50
Last Days of a Grading Period	51
When Grades are Posted	51
Fundraisers	52

Contents

Class Parties	53
Open House	54
Dress Up Days	54
Cold and Flu Season	55
Sick Day	56
The Weeks before Winter Break	56
Returning after a Break	57
Snow Day	58
Class Performance	59
Field Trip	60
Spring Fever	61
Standardized Testing	62
Awards Assemblies	63
End of a School Year	64
Summer Break	65
Professional Development	66
Introduction to Prayers for Entering the Classroom	69
ENTERING THE CLASSROOM	**71**
Every Day	71
Before the First Day	71
On the First Day of School	72
My First Year	73
After Many Years	73
My Last Year	74
After Maternity Leave	75
In a New Grade Level	76
At a New Campus	76
When I Have a Student Teacher	77
After a Conflict at Home	78
After Divorce	78
When Life at Home is Hard	79
While Grieving	79
When I Am Tired	80

Contents

When I Don't Feel Well	80
When I have Morning Sickness	80
When All is Good	81
When I'm Worried	81
When I'm Afraid	82
On My Birthday	82
When There's Nowhere I'd Rather Be	83
With Mindfulness	83
In Conflict with a Colleague	84
After a Difficult Meeting	84
After an Attack on a School	85
When Schools are in the Spotlight	86
After a Difficult Parent Conference	86
Near a Holiday	86
On a Rainy Day	87
On the First Snowy Day	88
The Last Day of School	89
Introduction to Prayers for the Community	93
PRAYERS FOR THE COMMUNITY	**95**
For the Ones Who Make Decisions	95
For the Custodial Staff	95
For the School Administrators	96
For the Office Staff	96
For the Cafeteria Staff	97
For the Counselor Who Tends to Children's Hearts	98
For the Counselor Who Coordinates Schedules and Testing	98
For the School Nurse	99
For the Instructional Coaches	100
For Our Faculty	100
For My Team	101
For the Colleague I Dislike	102
For the Colleague Who is Struggling	102

Contents

For the Colleague I Depend On	102
For the Substitute Teacher	103
For the Student Teacher	104
For My Class	104
For My Class When I Am Absent	105
For a Student on Her Birthday	106
For a Student Who Is Sick	106
For a New Student	107
For a Student Who Is Moving	107
For the Student Whose Parents Are Struggling	108
For a Bully	108
For a Student Who Is Bullied	109
For the Marginalized	110
For the English Language Learner	110
For the Child Who is Abused	111
For Parents Who are Abusive	112
For the Family with Economic Needs	112
For the Parent Volunteers	113
For the Parents Who Can't Volunteer	113
For the Families at School Events	114
For the Overextended Family	114
For the Family Experiencing Divorce	114
For the Critics	115
For My Family	116
For My Teachers	117
Introduction to Prayers of Lament	121
PRAYERS OF LAMENT	**123**
Fear and Worry	**123**
Change of Leadership	123
Long Absence	123
Angry Parent	124
I Am Moving	124
Budget Cuts	126

Contents

Anger and Frustration	**127**
Animosity toward a Colleague	127
When Lies Are Told about Me	128
When a Child is Abused or Neglected	128
Difficult Class	130
Ready to Quit (1)	131
Ready to Quit (2)	132
Poor Evaluation	133
Frustration with my Low Position	134
Overwhelmed by Work	135
Unjust System	136
Ineffective Leader	137
Disregard for My Health	138
My Salary	140
Bored by the Work	140
Grief and Sadness	**141**
My Beloved Colleague Is Leaving	141
My Beloved Principal Is Leaving	142
Loneliness	143
Missing My Children	144
Shelter in Place Drills	144
Confession	**145**
I Lost My Temper	145
Circumstances out of My Control	146
Comparison (1)	146
Comparison (2)	146
Self-Doubt	147
When Work Becomes Toil	148
When Work Becomes My Identity	149

Contents

Introduction to Breath Prayers	153
BREATH PRAYERS	**155**
On My Drive to School	155
When I'm Late to School	155
When I Step into My Classroom	155
During Breakfast in the Classroom	155
During Announcements	155
For Leading a Class down the Hall	155
Before a Lesson	156
While Grading	156
While Lesson Planning	156
During Standardized Testing	156
Before Checking My Email	156
Before Responding to an Email	156
For Looking at Student Data	156
When a Student has a Breakthrough	157
When a Student Is Disruptive	157
When a Class Is Disruptive	157
When a Student Shows Compassion	157
When a Student Is Unkind	157
While Students Work Independently	157
When I Get a New Student	157
When I Get a New Student (2)	157
For Waiting at the Restroom	158
In a Moment of Silence	158
When I Don't Feel Well	158
When I Need to Go to the Restroom but Can't	158
When a Child Vomits	158
When I Want to Quit	158
When Passing the Cafeteria	158
During a Fire Drill	158
Unsticking Zippers and Tying Shoes	159
A Read Aloud	159
Drinking Coffee	159

Contents

Hand Washing	159
Interrupted by the Intercom	159
For Dismissal	159
During Bus Duty	159
Waiting for Students to Be Picked Up	159
For a Parent Conference	160
In a Faculty Meeting	160
For Tutoring	160
While I Clean My Classroom	160
When I Leave the Building	160
On My Drive Home	160
Waves of Feeling	161
Postscript	*163*
Notes	*164*
About the Author	*166*
About the Artist	*167*

Acknowledgments

Many thanks to the people who helped get this book into the world. Thank you to the ACU students-turned-colleagues, the Friday Group (Ally, Rachael, and Michelle), Cari, Stephanie, and Dana for believing in this project and offering ideas and encouragement along the way. Thank you to Ellen (@ellenm.consulting) for her impeccable editing work, and to Dawn for getting the manuscript from my hard drive to these pages. Thank you, Eric, for creating beautiful artwork.

Forever love and gratitude to my husband, John, for always telling me to go for it, and to my kids, just for being.

Introduction

Dear Teacher,

I've been there.

I've felt the exhilaration of watching a reluctant reader getting lost in a book for the first time. I've also cried in my parked car, wondering whether I could make it through another day.

As a classroom teacher, I experienced the cycles of joy and sorrow. As an instructional coach, I worked beside both novice and veteran teachers, developing each person's capacity to thrive. As a university professor, I tried to prepare my students for the often difficult reality that awaited them. Teaching is a hard job. Knowledge, skills, and professional dispositions are essential to successful performance, but it takes more than that to persist.

It's likely you felt drawn, perhaps even called, to the classroom because you had a love for children. The scary secret we keep is that teaching is also loving parents, colleagues, and administrators and meetings, assessments, and class parties. Without a love big enough to cover it all, bitterness takes root and withers the teacher's heart.

I believe love of that scope comes from a higher power, but I know from experience that even when we turn to God in gratitude or lament, we may not have the words to express what we need in the moment.

I wrote these words for you, my friends and colleagues. They are not platitudes, but rather authentic prayers that emerged from years of teaching and working beside teachers. You can read them out loud or

in silence, alone or in community. Some are short enough to memorize while others are meant for longer meditation. To help you find the prayer you need, the book is divided into six sections.

- **Liturgies for Common Work** are for the mundane, the ordinary, and the everyday. The section contains short prayers, meant to focus your mind for the work you must do and do again, such as grading papers or checking your email. It also includes a prayer for each day of the week.

- **Blessings for Seasons** are prayers for special events such as field trips and class parties, as well as significant undertakings such as standardized testing.

- **Prayers for Entering the Classroom** recognize that we teach who we are. When it's your birthday, or you've left your newborn for the first time, or you've had a fight with your partner, these prayers guide you as you cross the threshold between the world at large and the work of the classroom.

- **Prayers for the Community** give voice to the need to love your neighbors and provide the words to pray for students, parents, and colleagues. When you need to pray for a challenging colleague, a student who is bullied, or a family who is struggling, this is where you can turn.

- **Prayers of Lament** provide solace on the days that leave you frustrated, angry, and despairing. They are honest about the brokenness of the world and the work, and yet proclaim God's ultimate sovereignty.
- **Breath Prayers** can be said in a moment. They can be easily memorized and on your lips when leading your class down the hall, during announcements, or in a fleeting moment of silence.

May the Lord bless you and keep you in the classroom,
Sheila Quinn

LITURGIES FOR

Common Work

INTRODUCTION TO

Liturgies for Common Work

Dear Teacher,

The hardest part of many good works is that they are never finished. I prepare meals for my family every day, but when they wake up in the morning, they are hungry again. I exercise to build my body's strength and endurance, but I can never say, "Now that I have that done, I don't have to exercise anymore." I repent of my sins, only to find that I am once again a sinner.

Your school day is full of repetitive tasks. The attendance must be taken every morning. (Don't forget!) You write lesson objectives, respond to emails, and grade papers. Again. And again.

If you feel called to teaching, particularly as a way to minister to others, you may not consider making copies or completing the lunch count to be holy work. We all like to imagine those life-changing moments that would make a good movie scene or the best chapter in our memoirs.

The problem is that those movie-worthy moments don't come around very often. In speaking of the daily work of caring, author Andi Ashworth said that "much of this labor is invisible to others, and because of this, it's often left out of our conversations about work, calling, and individual contributions to the common good of society."[1] In the same way, the daily preparation and processes required for good teaching aren't the stuff of interesting conversation or inspirational social media feeds.

Regardless of the lack of public appeal, repetition does not make these tasks less important. You may feel your spirit wither when faced with these tasks, but it is in such mundane work that you might also find life. Poet and essayist Kathleen Norris claimed that "in worship, as in human love, it is in the routine and the everyday that we find the possibilities for the greatest transformation."[2]

A liturgy is a ritual form of worship, and while *liturgy and ritual* may sound lofty, they imply routine and repetition. Liturgies such as the Lord's Prayer or the Eucharist are never finished and put aside, but repetition does not diminish their significance. Still, as Norris wrote, "it is not easy to maintain faith, hope or love in the everyday."

My desire is that this collection of prayers will reveal the sacred in your everyday tasks, so that you can recognize the ways your routine takes the shape of worship as everyday liturgies.

The Lord bless you and keep you,
Sheila

Liturgies for Common Work

For Another Day

Dear Lord,
I thank you for a new day.
May you rule in this classroom as you do in heaven.
Renew my heart and restore my energy.
Let me greet my students with love, erasing the record of
 yesterday's wrongs.
Give me a voice of kindness and patience.
Humble my pride and soften my heart.
Let me live each day with confidence that your kingdom is near.
Amen.

Sunday

God of all days,
I find you on Sunday morning
in the communion of saints,
over coffee and donuts,
communal worship,
and the Holy Eucharist.
You are with me on Sunday
 afternoons
for lingering lunches,
sports on T.V.,
and books that lead to naps.

The enemy finds me
as afternoon turns to evening.
It tells me I did not do enough,
questions the time I spent in rest,
and makes me fearful of the work I
must resume in the morning.
Grant that I may hear your voice
over my dread,
that I can be still
and know that you are God.
Amen.

Monday
Your love is steadfast, O Lord, and your mercies are new every morning. Forgive me when I groan as the world does, forgetting the blessing of meaningful work. Teach me to receive this new week with a renewed heart so that I may complete what was left undone, make right what went wrong, and begin the new tasks laid before me.
Amen.

Tuesday
Almighty God, thank you for another day to work. Bless our time for teaching and learning. May it be pleasing to you.
Amen.

Wednesday
Lord, I'm weary, yet rest is days away. Let me draw life from you. May my work be good and bring you glory.
Amen.

Thursday
Sustain me, Lord. The week is long. Forgive my tendency to quit before the task is done. Renew my spirit so that I may work wholeheartedly.
Amen.

Friday
Father of mercy, thank you for this day that is special because we've called it so. The clothes, the food, and the greetings all signal that the weekend is coming. Train my mind on the work that remains so that I can receive Sabbath unencumbered.
Amen.

Saturday

Lord of the Sabbath,
you rested on the seventh day;
you delivered the Israelites from bondage;
and you say that I am beloved.

Teach me to recognize when my work is done,
resist becoming a slave to my job,
and trust that my worthiness comes from you.
Lead me to rest.
Amen.

Greeting Students before Class

God, thank you for these first encounters.
For the students anxious to come in
and those who delay entry for as long as possible.
For the high fives, fist bumps, hugs, and shrugs;
the smiles, skips, and eyes that light up;
and also the yawns, rolling eyes, and dragging feet.
For the eye contact and averted gazes
that communicate different needs.
Teach me how to connect with the students who avoid connection.
May I give my best self to all of my students
from our first encounter to the end of the day.
Amen.

Lunch Count

Jesus, your disciples took a lunch count that day on the hill and worried there would not be enough food. That happens here too sometimes. I pray that our count is accurate, that each child's request will be granted, and that there will be enough for everyone who goes through the line.
Amen.

Morning Meeting

Lord, as we come together this morning, bless our community of learners. We have gathered from different places with joy and worry mingling in our hearts. Fill this space with a spirit of authenticity and love. May we all extend grace to each other so that this circle is a safe space for honest sharing. Quiet our worries and insecurities. Set our intentions on gratitude, beauty, and good work.
Amen.

Taking Attendance

Dear God, Thank you for the gift of each child's presence today.
Be with those who are out sick, without a ride, or doing other things.
Watch over those who will join us later, whether frantic and rushing or sleeping through alarms that never seem to work properly.
Whether on time or after a reminder, I thank you for the chance to consider those whom you have placed in my midst.
Amen.

Pacing

Dear God,
It is hard to know how the plans I put on paper will translate to the clock. You know my students do not concern themselves with time.

Show me where to linger and when to move along.
Let me be clear, but not short; concise, but not rushed; thorough,
  but not redundant.
Give me the skill of thinking on my feet, navigating and redirecting the lesson as I go, rather than attempting to stay locked into predetermined plans. Help me recognize what is essential, what can be cut, and what needs more time on another day. May I continue to grow in this area for the good of my students.
Amen.

Before Teaching a Math Lesson

Holy Creator, The earth displays your thoughtfulness.
May I convey the splendor of all the numbers, shapes, and patterns in our world.
I pray that I will not reduce beauty to the recitation of facts
or limit wonder to the completion of algorithms.
Instead, let me invite my students to marvel at the order of infinity.
Amen.

Before Teaching a Language Arts Lesson

God of words,
By speaking,
you created the earth and all
   that is in it.
From Word you became flesh
and dwelled among us.
By your words people were healed
and the Good News spread.
You gave us songs to sing,
laws to live by,
and stories
of your love for us.

Thank you for the gifts of
listening and speaking,
reading and writing,
questioning and thinking.

As you demonstrated in the
   beginning,
in your time on earth,
and in the Word you left us:
literacy is more than drills,
   worksheets,
or multiple-choice answers.
Remind me,
as I teach the language arts,
that language is powerful.

Keep my eyes open to the
   responsibility
I've been given.
Let me shine the light of words
throughout my lesson.
Amen.

Before Teaching a Science Lesson
God of the universe, thank you for giving us minds that love to explore and endless space for exploration. As we study the science of energy, elements, earth, and living things, grant us postures of humility.

I pray that each discovery leads our hearts closer to you. Protect us from the illusion that we have learned our way beyond our need for You. As we explore answers, let us be mindful of the questions that matter. May our search for understanding remind us that the world is vast and remarkable by design. Grant us understanding without hubris and curiosity without chaos.
Amen.

Before Teaching a Social Studies Lesson
Dear Lord, as I invite my students to explore the world we live in and the people who interact with it, give me wisdom. It is tempting to skip over these lessons for the sake of time or for fear of wading into the inherent messiness. Through, and at times despite, this curriculum, may we learn how to care for each other and the world you've entrusted to us. May our social studies bring forth your kingdom.

The study of geography, history, economics, and government is inextricably tied to stories of power, oppression, greed, and suffering. But it also includes people who worked toward justice. Show me how to convey it all with humility, grace, and gratitude. Give me courage to tell the world's story honestly, admitting that I do not understand it all and that I do not have answers for the problems that have plagued us since our exile from the Garden. Only, *Your kingdom come. Your will be done, on earth as in heaven.*
Amen.

Lunch

God of mercy, give me rest. Bless these moments of peace while my students are out of my care.

Help me choose stillness over commotion,

truth over gossip, and

kindness over pride.

May the words of my mouth and the meditations of my heart be pleasing to you.

And may the food I eat, however meager or abundant, nourish my body for the work ahead.

Amen.

Recess

Lord,

Let them be daring, collecting bruises that will make them stronger and wiser.

Let them be generous, reaching out to the child who stands alone.

Let them be pure in heart, resisting gossip and dirty jokes.

Let them be courageous, standing up for the least of these.

Let me be their model, Lord, and forgive me when I forget.

Amen.

Coming in from Recess

God,

Thank you for our time to play, and bless our return to work. Help us transition quickly, with focus and positive intentions. May the panting breaths, rosy cheeks, and sweaty-head smell dissipate quickly.

Amen.

Reading Aloud

We praise you,
God of words.
Out of your imagination
and from your voice,
you made the earth.

We reenact such creativity
by reading stories
and sharing art
in community.

Bless the ears that hear the words
and the eyes that absorb the images.
May my selection be worthy
of our time together.

Breathe your life into my voice
so that my students may experience
the fullness of an encounter
with goodness and truth.
Amen.

Guided Reading

Father, bless this table and the children who gather here. Thank you for providing a space and a means to meet their needs. May they integrate the sounds, symbols, and fluency that bring life to silent words on the page; may I give them access and invitation to the community of readers; and may they recognize the power and joy of its membership.
Amen.

Stations

God of all spaces,
I have assembled tasks and activities for my students to complete in
    orderly ways.
Lord, I pray that we have kind words and cooperative spirits;
that the materials I've chosen are high quality, able to endure the
manipulation of many hands;
that my instructions are clear, encouraging independence;
and that the content is rigorous, meeting their needs and making the
    most of our instructional day.
May the picture in my classroom match the one in my imagination.
Amen.

LAMINATING MATERIALS

God, I pray your blessing on the laminator.

It demonstrates humankind's ingenuity and limitations. We've devised a way to make delicate materials durable, a feeble grab at immortality. Yet without a heavy clip, the film feeds back into the machine, reminding us that we are not gods after all.

I pray that the film is sufficient and loaded correctly; that the machine is on, freed from its "out of order" sign, and heated sufficiently; that my glue is good, neither creating wet streaks nor leaving pages to peel apart. Give me the patience to feed my materials slowly, avoiding both overlap and wastefully wide gaps.

Amen.

MAKING COPIES

Lord, bless the copy machine and my time in its presence. I pray that it is fully functioning and that the line is short. Remind me to be kind to the person ahead of me with the year's supply of math worksheets to copy, collate, and staple. And may I be generous to the one behind me who only needs to "run a few, real quick."

I pray that the toner holds out, the manual feed stays attached, and Zone B is without distress. Spare me from jammed paper, error messages, and black streaks across stacks of pages. If that is not to be, let me find the source quickly and without anger.

Have mercy on me, oh Lord, I pray.
Amen.

Giving Children Internet Access
God of the universe, there is so much in the world, both beautiful and vile.

All of it can be found on the Internet.

Protect these children as I give them access to the world outside of our classroom. Keep me alert and diligent, committed to protecting their hearts and minds from those who would do them harm. I pray they will be compliant with my instructions and committed to their own technology use agreements.

Teach us all to be wise.
Amen.

Instructional Technology
I have come to depend on the technology in my room for everything from grading to student engagement. May the tools I've chosen make my teaching more effective and not merely flashy.

Bless the tangle of cords and the invisible path of Bluetooth connection;
bless the Internet access that keeps me connected to my content, my students, and their families,
bless the batteries and lightbulbs, unsung heroes of our digital age.
In times of trouble, I pray that "turn it off, turn it back on" is sufficient.

Lord, forgive me when I depend on technology more than on you.
Amen.

Redirecting a Student

Father in heaven,

Teach me your ways.
When a student does not meet
the expectations of our classroom
I am tempted to speak and act
reflexively.

Search my heart, oh Lord.
If there is anything self-serving
    or shaming,
let your spirit move in me,
so that I may balance justice
    and mercy,
speak sparingly,
and be reflective.

You taught us that discipline
is a demonstration of love.
I pray this is true in my classroom.
That every correction serves
    to encourage,
not to conquer.

May my redirection be kind
    and firm,
for the edification of the child,
not an outburst of my own
    insecurity.
May I remain in the position
    of a teacher
and avoid attempts at
manipulation or control.
Amen.

Library Day

God of the universe,

As my students visit the library today,
open their eyes to wonder at the world you have created.
Through fiction, let them learn empathy and wholeheartedness.
Through nonfiction, let them see that the world is vast.
Above all, let them recognize your sovereignty;
the greater the world is, the greater you must be.
Amen.

Packing Up at the End of the Day
As the students prepare to leave, I thank you again for meaningful work.
Bless the hands that gather trash and stack the chairs.
May all the folders, coats, and lunchboxes find their way home.
Prepare the hearts and homes that will welcome them next.
Amen.

As My Students Leave
Dear God, thank you for the close of another day with my students. Keep them safe as they scatter from the boundaries and predictability of the school day. Give them blessings of food, shelter, and love while they are away. Guard them through the night.
Amen.

After the Students Are Gone
As I stand in the transition from one part of my work to the next, give me peace. I am tired. The worries and victories of the day compete for my attention. Forgive me for the wrongs I've committed, things done and left undone. Calm the chaos. Train my thoughts on gratitude.

Give me the discernment to know what is urgent, what is essential, and what is extraneous. Let me prioritize what needs to be done well and what simply needs to get done, so that I can go home with energy left for the other loves in my life.
Amen.

Tutoring
God, it's hard to know what purpose this extra time will serve. I confess that at times it seems futile, and I wonder if the students feel the same way. It's hard to face another hour. We are tempted to give up; help us persist.

Let me show up in the way my students need.
Amen.

Faculty Meetings
Dear God,
Thank you for community. As we come together, set our minds on our common purpose. Remind us of the importance of our work and the priorities we should set.

Give me a heart of hospitality. Let my countenance, posture, and words be welcoming to those around me. Quiet the voice reminding me of the many things I need to do, could be doing now, so that I can be fully present. Set my mind on the information and the intent of the presenter.

Let us live in peace, speaking and listening in ways that sharpen one another, and may our disagreements clarify our path.

Thank you for meaningful work.
Amen.

Before Reading Emails
Lord of my life, I come to you. You are my rock and my salvation.

My inbox contains predictability and possibility waiting in a sans serif list. Teach me to use this tool wisely. Narrow my intention and set my mind on productivity.

Where there are demands, let me respond with calm energy.
Where there are questions, let me respond with wisdom.
Where there is anger, let me respond with kindness.
Where there is ignorance, let me respond with grace.
Where there is generosity, let me respond with gratitude.

When I close my inbox with a longer to-do list, give me energy to accomplish the work you have set before me.
Amen.

IEP Meetings

God, I know you care deeply for those who struggle. Make me like you.

Bless this room and the people gathered in it.

We need counselors and specialists who are prepared and committed.
We need parents who have the courage to speak honestly and listen generously.
We need teachers who value all perspectives.
We need administrators who are present and undistracted.

Help us listen, not only to words, but also to the feelings, intentions, and souls of those gathered. May we work with one heart and mind in the best interest of the child.

Give us wisdom to see the data clearly and use it to build paths for success. We want our student to develop agency and responsibility, alongside academic growth. To that end, help us make decisions that are best for today and will serve for a lifetime.
Amen.

Virtual Meetings

Lord,
I come to you before our virtual meeting. I pray that the software and Internet work as designed and that everyone who needs to be in attendance knows how to log in and does so on time. May our connection be strong and our batteries sufficiently charged. If my face must freeze, grant me the mercy of looking pleasantly engaged and not perpetually confused or annoyed.
Amen.

On Social Media
God, bless my time on social media.
On the network before me, there is no limit to the audience who may have access to the content I create. Likewise, I have granted many voices entry into my thoughts. *May I refrain from anything dehumanizing, dishonest, or destructive.*

In the content I consume, let me be discerning, never believing that anyone is as wrong or as right as they appear in a handful of characters, a grid of images, or a video clip. *May I dwell on whatever is pure, lovely, or trustworthy.*

In the content I create, give me discretion. I speak for myself, but I represent many. In this moment, I am particularly aware of the students, parents, and community members who may be impacted by the words I say, the photos I share, and the comments I leave.

May your work of redemption be done online as it is on earth.
Amen.

Virtual Class
God,
I'll begin by taking attendance, but what does it mean to be present when we are not together?

When vanity tempts us to look at our reflections rather than each other,
when a parade of siblings, parents, and pets crosses the screen,
when we're given a window into bedrooms and kitchens,
when there are features to explore and backgrounds to try,
increase my creativity,
focus our attention,
and energize us for learning.
Amen.

Before Calling a Parent

Father and Mother of all,
search my heart before I dial.
Erase my pride and the insecurity
    it masks.
Set my intentions on what is true,
    noble, and right.
Give me courage and compassion
    in equal measure.
Keep me present in the
    conversation,
committed to listening,
slow to speak,
and slow to anger.
Amen.

Lesson Planning

God of creation, you brought order from chaos. I am your image
bearer; bless my creative work.

As you separated day from night and land from sea, so may I establish
    the depth and breadth of material before me.

As you filled the earth with life, so may my lessons be purposeful
    and engaging.

As you looked at creation and called it good, so may I take pleasure
    in my work.

Amen.

Grading Papers

Thank you, God, for the work of my students and their demonstration
of understanding. May I honor their efforts with my time and response.

Grant me the energy to complete the task in a timely manner and the
stamina to see the last one as I saw the first.

Give me eyes to see strengths before weaknesses, both in my students
and in myself. Guard my heart against shame or shaming. Fill me with
wisdom and grace.

Let me see in their work the path we should take.
Amen.

Displaying Student Work
Dear Lord,
I'm putting student work on display, artifacts of our time and effort in the classroom. In it, I see evidence of things my students have accomplished for the first time and the promise of what they are ready to do next. I pray that others see the same.

As I select samples to share, may I honor the hearts of my students. I pray that every showcase provides motivation through inspiration and never by shame. My desire is for my choices to reflect the best my students have to offer, highlighting growth, not perfection. Help me resist the temptation to display work for self-congratulation. If I boast, let it be in your grace.

Putting work samples on display invites the temptation to compare. When students see their work hanging next to their classmates', pride may be diminished by the recognition of differences. I am not immune, as I wonder whether our work measures up to the class down the hall. Guard our hearts, Lord.
Amen.

Time Management
Lord, it is hard to manage my time; the day requires so much.

Every task feels equally necessary, including unimportant demands disguised in urgent. Give me discernment to order my day. Let me put aside the distractions and avoid choosing what is easy over what is meaningful. Help me recognize the difference between what needs to be done for my students and what I do for show. Help me balance the need to connect with my community and the need to close my door.

May I be grateful for the time you've given me rather than grieving what I've lost. Teach me to be a good steward of your gift. May I be gracious with myself and extend such grace to others.
Amen.

BOUNDARIES FOR MY TIME
Have mercy on me, Lord.

Everything I try to leave at work is only a ringtone away. When I hear temptation's call, I respond as though every matter is urgent. In my arrogance or insecurity, I can't resist a quick look that turns into an evening of constant vigilance and rapid response. When I can't take action before the new workday begins, my mind stores up worries for the morning.

Give me the courage I need to set boundaries. Do not let me be overcome by illusions of loyalty or productivity. Show me where to draw the lines for myself and others, so that I may serve you well.
Amen.

SENSE OF HUMOR
God, grant me a sense of humor. As I go through long days and quick years, reveal the absurd, silly, and strange. Let me choose joy, even as I struggle. Remind me how funny my students are. Teach me to see the comedy inherent in our attempts to work together daily. Show me the world through their eyes, where so many things are worthy of laughter. Let me take time to laugh, even when I have work to do. Bring light and levity to this serious work.
Amen.

Blessings for Seasons

INTRODUCTION TO

Blessings for Seasons

Dear Teacher,

One of my teaching partners used to bring me a cup of hot chocolate and a cinnamon roll on the morning of the year's first freeze. She knew I would grumble at the ice on my windshield, the biting wind on the walk from the parking lot, and the seasonal loss of outdoor recess. I've never been a winter person.

Like nature, school years also cycle through seasons. And just as nature turns from winter to spring, then summer, then fall, the school year has its own periods of novelty, routine, stress, and relief. The general public is aware of our patterns of back to school, spring break, and summer vacation. Teachers know that there are also seasons of fundraising, parent conferences, and standardized testing.

Some of these seasons feel like the freshness of spring, when everything comes alive and is full of possibility. Others are more like winter, when darkness seems to get more than its due. While you may have a favorite, none of the four seasons is inherently better or worse than another. Each one has unique significance in the greater story of creation. Likewise, each season in the school calendar serves a purpose in the lives of our schools and students. Seasons are both natural and sacred. They come and go with such regularity that we sometimes forget that life, death, and rebirth are miraculous.

The prayers in this section follow the general flow of the school year, with the understanding that some seasons might fall on different pages in your calendar. My hope is that with a few tweaks to the order, you can pray your way through the school year, accepting and surrendering to each season as you do.

The Lord bless you and keep you,
Sheila

Blessings for Seasons

SETTING UP A CLASSROOM

To the One who spoke the universe into being, lead me as I prepare the place to live and learn with my students.

You organized the world into night and day and separated the land from the sea. In the same way, let me set boundaries in the classroom, designating homes for materials and people so that we feel safe in the predictability of our space and schedule.

You created a world that meets our needs. From the earth we get our food, shelter, and clothing. So too let me provide access to the supplies we will need to cultivate our minds.

You imagined a world that is unnecessarily beautiful, communicating your love in sunsets, ocean waves, and flowers. In the same way, let me fill our classroom with wonder and hospitality for all who enter.

After six days of work, you called creation good and rested. So let me be pleased with a job well done and allow myself Sabbath before our year begins.
Amen.

Meet the Teacher Night
Holy God,
In the midst of our preparations for another school year, we have set aside time to meet each other. I know their names, and they know mine. Some are familiar, and others are unknown. Excitement and nervousness will swirl about the room, my own emotions reflected on their faces.

Bless the parents who enter. *Their* children are *my* students, and we will negotiate these distinct roles and shared love over the coming months.
May we be willing to extend grace to each other.

Bless the students who enter. Weeks of expectation are expressed in nervous handshakes, hugs, or hiding.
May they enter with confidence.

Bless our new classroom. We are a gathering of strangers, brought together by external forces. Through the year, we will share life and transformation.
May this be the place where we all find belonging.
Amen.

Beginning of a School Year
Lord, it is not a day or a week, but a season. It began even before the previous year ended, as I collected "maybe next year" dreams on sticky notes and Pinterest boards. It continued in the summer when I set aside time to turn those ideas into concrete plans. Even now that the preparation is complete and we all—students, parents, and teachers—have been introduced, the newness lingers. Bless our beginning of the school year.

Grant me patience as I teach the routines and procedures that will be the foundation of safety and productivity every day that we're together. Let me lean on my skills as a teacher to manage my class, trusting that I will watch my students learn to work together. Renew my persistence daily, setting aside time to review and practice, even beyond the time when they first demonstrate success.

In the hustle to complete assessments, may I recognize the value of the data to guide my decisions. Expand my view beyond the numbers. Give me a full picture of each child as a whole human, not the average of a spreadsheet column.

Perform a miracle on our paperwork, mighty God. I pray that parents can navigate the online system and submit accurate information. I pray that all students return their folders with the forms completed and signed. I pray that I find a way to keep track of it all so that deadlines are met and I can get on with the business of teaching.

Open my eyes to those in need: the students who will say for weeks that they "forgot" their supplies, the first-year teacher whose desperate smile betrays the truth of her struggle, and the new members of our staff who are anxious to demonstrate their competence and may not speak their questions out loud.

Make me your servant, Lord.
Amen.

Parent-Teacher Conferences

Lord, it is the time of the year when I will meet with the parents and guardians of all my students. I will sit on this side of the threshold while they file in, listen to my prepared monologue, and file out.

There is information that must be shared with everyone. Help me to remember that though I've said it many times, it is all new for the person in front of me. When I must share information specific to individual students, let me speak with compassion. When speaking about someone's child, there is always danger of offense. They love their children fiercely, at times recklessly, and I must balance gentleness with truth. Let me avoid tiptoeing but show kindness through clarity. Make my care evident though my words and tone.

Be with the families as they make arrangements to meet. Clear their paths for childcare, time away from work, and transportation. May they feel welcomed as they enter our building and confident as they come into our classroom.

I pray that our season of meetings is productive and more than routine. May we all find value and discovery in the time we spend together. *Amen.*

The Longest Stretch

Lord, bless the stretch of time from Labor Day to Thanksgiving.

Thank you for this season of minimal interruptions. We have collected the paperwork, attended the trainings, and are finally left alone to do our jobs of teaching and learning. The fervor of the new school year has died down, and we are not yet assailed by the holiday season. The routine and schedule are unchanged from one day to the next, making our days full and predictable.

Thank you for revealing my students' needs to me. The minutes are spent productively, making progress toward new learning rather than identifying or trying to fill gaps from the previous year. We are in our content now. I've had time to learn their habits and patterns. I know what sets them off and what keeps them going. I have met many of their parents and learned about their brothers, sisters, and sitters. Indeed, we have become our own family inside the walls of this classroom.

Thank you for making me known to my students. They know what to expect and how to accomplish what is needed for the day. They understand my humor and respond to my changes in tone. They are comfortable with each other and have practiced the norms of our community. They operate efficiently and independently in this space, because it has become their own.

Thank you for a season of learning without test preparation. Of course, high stakes, disguised as accountability, always loom on the horizon, but for now, the threat is kept at bay. We can relish the excitement of discovery, practice without penalty, and be experimental in our approaches.

There is much to love about this season, Lord, but it is not without vulnerability. The excitement of the new year wears off, and monotony threatens to take over. Without care, every day will look like the one before, not only in structure, but also in substance. Without vigilance, the intentionality of the first weeks will fade into sluggishness. Spark my creativity and call me into the fullness of the life you've given us to share in this space. May I make the most of these autumn days.
Amen.

Picture Day

Reminders to remove glasses
    and coats,
wipe faces,
and smooth hair.
Line up according to height,
Awkward smiles,
and tilted chins,
but not too much.
One, two, three
and the moment
is captured.
This class,
these faces,
this moment.
God bless picture day.
Amen.

Assembly

God, there are times when it is good for us to assemble in large groups. From the youngest to the oldest, we will meet for a common purpose.

Our togetherness creates unique energy. This is not our classroom; the norms of our routine have been disrupted. Under the presumed cover of a crowd, some students will grow more daring. Others will become anxious as the noise and the vitality press against them. I will be on heightened alert, aware that I will be judged by my students' behavior and my ability to respond. Even so, please use this time to strengthen our school community.

Someone has the charge of speaking into this mix. I pray they are prepared and that their message is edifying and able to be heard by all. And may they finish on time so that we can get back to our classrooms. *Amen.*

Last Days of a Grading Period
Lord, I am pressed on every side.

My desk and my mind are occupied by coffee, calculations, and a row of open tabs on my screen. I attempt to finish grading at the same time that students submit make-up work and corrections. I have emails from the office reminding me to submit grades, from parents asking about an assignment posted four weeks ago, and from students making their case for scores they need but did not earn. Even as I close out this grading period, I am preparing new lessons and assignments for next week.

I need energy, courage, and patience to finish this course. Deliver me to a new day, Lord.
Amen.

When Grades are Posted
God, thank you for the conclusion of another grading period.

I pray that my assessments were valid,
the calculations accurate,
and the reporting clear.

I am weary yet aware that finalizing grades is an invitation to questions and critique.
Sustain my mind and spirit in the presence of both.
Amen.

Fundraisers

In this season of fundraising, we manipulate our students' optimism and desire to belong. A hype man instills in them the importance of doing their part. Spurred on by trinkets that will be lost or broken within the week, they will venture out. When the first in my class receives her "collectible" knickknack, it will kick off an ambitious sales streak.

Lord, forgive us.

They will solicit neighbors, grandparents, and parents' coworkers. We will advise them against approaching strangers, but they're often undeterred. Protect them as they venture out. May people support their efforts, whether motivated by guilt, generosity, or the quickest way to get them off the stoop.

Lord, forgive us.

Our students will carry forms, catalogues, and boxes, like the Kirby and Britannica reps of the past. We send them into the sunshine with bars of chocolate or cartons of frozen cookie dough, hoping beyond reason that the products will make it to their patrons before oozing out of their packaging.

Lord, forgive us.

We dread this season. It reminds us how much time we spend on non-teaching tasks. Every morning we collect forms, count money, and send out reminders. While we acknowledge that there must be a better way, we haven't yet arrived at it.

Lord, forgive us.

People assume that tax revenue is sufficient, but we struggle to give our students what they need. We have oversized classes and undersized space, while parents clamor for the latest technology. Someone will say, when asked to support the local school by purchasing a tin of popcorn, that they already pay their taxes. The city and state's budget communicates its priorities.

Lord, help us.
Amen.

Class Parties

Parents and guests that I've never seen before will be present on this day.
Bless all who enter here.

Games, songs, and contests will replace the curriculum.
Bless our celebration.

Tables, faces, and probably the floor will be covered with cupcakes, cookies, and syrup-filled drinks.
Bless these symbols of feasting.

Shouts and laughter will spill out of the classroom.
Bless the voices of joy.

We'll clean it all in the wake of sugar and excitement.
Bless our return to ordinary time.
Amen.

Open House

Oh, Lord, we eagerly anticipate the arrival of our guests. We've disinfected, emptied desks, and filled trashcans. Everything has been put in order. Bless this space and all who enter it.

Our best work is on display. A curated collection representing our time, my teaching, and their learning.

When we all come together, school family and home families colliding in a small space, there is potential for awkwardness, resentment, and judgment. God, I beg you to clear my heart of malice. Teach me to welcome all who come with eyes to see love and fear in their many disguises. Let me handle myself with dignity and grace, shining a light that glorifies you.

May our guests see the students' work and progress without comparison so that pride doesn't become boastful and opportunities for growth don't become moments of shame. Let them recognize the displays for what they are: snapshots of particular moments in time.

Families, friends, and teachers demonstrate their love in different ways, at times overlapping. May the students revel in the joy of being surrounded by its many expressions.

You've promised that you are preparing a place for us and that we are all invited to your banquet. I pray that our open house is a reflection of that perfect gathering to come.
Amen.

Dress Up Days

To the God who stretched the necks of giraffes,
put eyes on the peacock's feathers,
and gave the turkey its wattle;
We give you praise for so much silliness.

You placed in us a desire for fun,
so now we arrive in socks with tassels,
ridiculous hats,
outrageous sunglasses,
and elaborate outfits from decades gone by.

When I am tempted to begrudge the shenanigans, teach me to embrace the joy. Remind me that children need frivolity, and perhaps I do too. Our pressures are so great, it can be difficult to allow time for amusement, but we need these moments to build community in our classroom and in our school. They are not wasteful.

When the silliness leads to misbehavior and distraction, keep me from grumbling. When I am tempted to throw in the towel on learning, help me resist. My students' success depends in part on my commitment to doing my job well every day. Restore my purpose and show me how to use their energy to my instructional advantage. It is not in vain.
Amen.

Cold and Flu Season

Lord, we come to you in our weakness.

From October to March, we are under microscopic assault, forced to recognize our limitations. The common cold and the flu-strep-mono triple threat linger in the air and on every desk, door, and pencil.

You made our bodies in miraculous ways. Though we live with the curse of disease, you've given us the mercy of defense. Give us wisdom as we treat our bodies with rest, nutrition, and medication. Bless the washing of hands, the wiping of tables, and the covering of sneezes.

May our vulnerability increase our faith. Protect us, Lord, we pray.
Amen.

Sick Day

Lord, I cannot go to school today; my body has reached its limit.

I pray that my preparations were sufficient, and my colleagues find the materials and instructions I've left for days like these. Thank you for the systems that will keep my students safe.

Lord, I pray that a substitute, kind and competent, is with my students today. But if they are split across the campus, may my colleagues be hospitable. If the class is covered by someone whose time in my room will leave another job undone, may they be forgiving.

In any circumstance, I pray that my students will be cooperative and respectful.

Heal me, Lord I pray.
Amen.

The Weeks before Winter Break

The signs are evident:
a tree twinkling in the corner of the classroom,
student performances,
class parties,
matching sweaters,
and goodies in the teacher's lounge.

We make ready for the day, Lord,
giving exams,
entering grades,
redirecting excited energy,
unplugging appliances,
and submitting final checklists.

In this Advent season,
give us an abundance
of patience,
persistence,
and deep breaths
as we wait
with hope and
expectation.
Amen.

Returning after a Break
God, as I return from the break, my emotions are mixed, but I will choose to walk in gratitude and faith.

Thank you for work that is meaningful;
I have faith that you will bless my offering to your kingdom.

Thank you for work that provides income;
I trust that you will provide what I need.

Thank you for the space to do this work;
I am confident that you will dwell with us.

Thank you for my students;
I am certain that you are working in their lives, beyond what I can see.

Thank you for seasons of work and rest;
I know that you will give me strength for the day.
Amen.

Snow Day

Thank you, God, for this miracle of light and reprieve! The lessons, meetings, and assemblies will wait. All is hushed by the blanketing snow.

I could carve out a warm spot and wrap myself in comfort,
act without urgency,
tending to my soul.

I could turn up the music that gets me moving,
satisfy the voices,
cross to-dos off lists.
I could engage with others,
sit without rushing,
nowhere else to be.

In rest, I catch my breath.
In productivity, I get caught up.
In community, I find myself.
In all, Lord, let me recover my heart.

Holy Guardian, keep my students safe as they explore and play.
Lead us back together, whole.
Amen.

Class Performance

Maker, we are gathered for a special occasion. Let me honor this singular moment, when this particular class will perform for an audience of those who love them most.

Thank you for the mix of emotions you've placed in our hearts and the way you've made our bodies to respond with what we need. Give each performer a quick recollection of their lines and movements. Let the props and special effects function flawlessly. Make our hours of preparation evident in the ease of our performance.

For this night, bring peace to the families of divorce, separation, or remarriage; to the generations, the friends, and the fringes. Cast aside their differences so that they can be united by love for their children on the stage.

Quiet the smallest ones in our audience. We are grateful they are here, part of our extended classroom family, and we pray they will be engaged and minimally distracting.
Thank you for the other faculty and administrators who were encouraged to be here but do not do so without sacrifice.

Thank you for the community assembled. May their time with us be blessed.
Amen.

Field Trip

I know that wherever we go, God, you are there. Today, as we leave the familiarity of our school building, have mercy on us.

For the bus ride with so many voices straining to be heard,
Lord have mercy.

For the driver who will spend the day with us, mostly waiting, mostly patiently,
Lord have mercy.

For the people who will greet us at our destination and guide our experience,
Lord have mercy.

For the parents who have volunteered to join us,
Lord have mercy.

For the premises and the areas both open and off-limits,
Lord have mercy.

For my students, eager and excited to break out of our routine,
Lord have mercy.

For the lessons they'll learn and the curiosity that is sparked,
Lord have mercy.

For me, with my agenda, emergency bag, and optimism,
Lord, have mercy.
Amen.

Spring Fever

God of the seasons, your creation tells our story. The birds, the flowers, and the sun burst forth after winter, declaring that death is only an illusion; resurrection has come!

Divine Maker, bless our spring fever.

Walking from the car to the classroom takes on a different feeling. In the winter, I duck my head and hurry to get inside. Now, I'm tempted to linger. I walk slowly, noticing the birdsong and new fragrance in the air.

The walls of the classroom seem oppressive. When I leave at the end of the day, I'm certain a million natural miracles have occurred in my absence. The world is suddenly vibrant; trees are fuller; grass is taller. And I missed it.

My students, too, seem keenly aware that we don't belong inside. They scoot in chairs, skip down halls, and chatter like the birds. Their focus shifts, and I struggle to create a sense of urgency about our work. Forgive me for pulling down the shades.

When they're not looking out the windows, they are looking at each other. Noticing, for the first time, that the boy or girl sitting across the room is especially interesting. Funny. Cute. Both sides attempting and failing to appear discreet or aloof.

It is a miraculous, yet hard season, Lord. Assessments must be completed, and curriculum standards must be met before spring turns to summer. Still, we are all keenly aware that creation is singing your glory, and we long to be part of the chorus.

Renew our purpose, Lord, and help us focus. May our longing for life and light remind us of our desire for you. Come soon, Lord Jesus. *Amen.*

Standardized Testing

Our God and Creator, be near us on these challenging days.

A collection of questions composed by strangers will claim to capture the depth and breadth of my students' learning.
May the test makers be sensitive to bias.

My students feel the weight of this day, even when they don't understand it.
May all children feel empowered to do their best.

I am anxious about the long-term impact these few hours of testing will have on curriculum, grade placement, and reputations.
May I find peace in things that abide: faith, hope, and love.

Standardization has potential to shine light on the shadows of inequity and demonstrate the achievements of students and teachers who have overcome the barriers of their circumstances.
May the scores bring about justice.
Amen.

Awards Assemblies
Awards Day is coming.
Lord, prepare my heart.

In the midst of celebrating the first, best, and most,
give me eyes to see the last and the least.

I will see students who are easy to reward, compliant with rules and bent toward achievement.
Turn my eyes toward the disenfranchised who face more barriers than opportunities.
I will see students in "Sunday best" with hairstyles we haven't seen since picture day.
Turn my eyes toward the one wearing the same clothes as the day before.

I will see students with a row of cheerleaders making the applause noticeably louder when their name is called.
Turn my eyes toward the ones who have no one listening for their names.

Teach me to acknowledge my students with presence more than certificates,
to value compassion over comparison,
and to honor good work without mistaking a child's achievement for her worth.
Amen.

End of a School Year

There are seasons that seem longer than the number of days assigned to it. Lord, how can we measure the end of a school year? We can feel its approach from weeks away, though at first it seems it will never arrive. And now, we are in the midst of the season, and the spinning, frenetic pace is dizzying.

There is so much to do between now and when we will rest. The lists go on and on, but the routines and structures that kept us well and made us productive throughout the year have evaporated. When I look at my calendar, I cannot find a "normal" day left. We have meetings, assemblies, testing, and events. They signal the end of the year yet make it seem impossible to reach.

Teach me to cherish the days remaining with my students. Make my love for them evident. May my countdown to the last day be a reminder that our time together is precious. Show me how to make the most of these final days, to teach them that they have value and to make sure their bodies, minds, and spirits are nourished. I pray that I can give them an academic boost that will carry them through the summer. Do not let me squander these moments in a rush to the summer break.

Lord, keep me from overwhelm. Remind me of the success I've had in the past. When I look at my to-do list, help me see it in manageable allotments. Let me leave no loose ends. Give me the energy to accomplish all that is required, the courage to have honest conversations, and the grace to do it all with my honor, sanity, and integrity intact.
Amen.

Summer Break

Thank you, God, for the gift of
summer break.

For days of leisure
without alarms
or rushing
out the door.

For the indulgence of twilight,
even on Sunday
when my heart quickens,
then relaxes.

For time to read
for pleasure,
by choice
and by recommendation.

For the privilege to travel,
to experience your world
with its wonder
and possibilities.

For opportunities to learn,
work, and stay connected
to my craft
and community.

For attention to home and family,
projects and promises
stacked in corners
until now.

Bless my feet where they walk,
and my mind where it wanders.
Renew my spirit
and make me whole.
Amen.

Professional Development

Lord, we've come for different reasons:
to equip ourselves to better serve our students,
to fulfill professional or legal requirements,
to make connections that may serve us later,
to get a free tote bag and long lunch.
Christ, grant the best of our intentions.

God, I confess that I am not always prepared to learn.
I am prideful about my own level of expertise;
I am cynical about the system that brought me here;
I am excited to catch up with friends and colleagues;
I am tempted to reach for distraction on a screen.
Christ, forgive my arrogance.

On this day, Lord, set my heart on gratitude
for the opportunity to grow,
for the system that affords me the opportunity,
for time with like-minded professionals,
for tote bags and long lunches.
Christ, bless our work.
Amen.

Prayers for Entering the Classroom

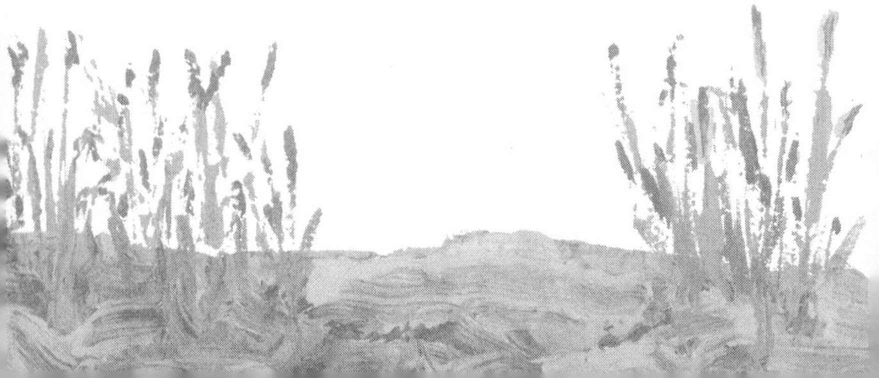

INTRODUCTION TO
Prayers for Entering the Classroom

Dear Teacher,

When I returned to work after my son was born, a student whispered to me after my first class, "I think your shirt is on backward." Sure enough, it was. I was sleep deprived and foggy-brained, and I'd gotten dressed in the dark to avoid waking the baby who was now sharing my bedroom.

No matter your season, the truth is that your identities, histories, and moods enter the classroom with you every day. Parker Palmer, educator and activist, says that "we teach who we are."[3] In this way, the classroom is a convergence of the public and private, personal and professional.

Of course, this convergence is both a blessing and a curse. On your best days, your energy can be enough to fuel an entire classroom. Some mornings feel sacred and significant, days to be marked with solemnity or celebration. At other times, your energy is scarcely enough to dress yourself properly. These are the days when it is all a teacher can do to drag herself across the threshold with the weight of the world on her shoulders.

Most days, though, are unremarkable. It is ordinary, after all, to have good days and bad ones, sickness and health, relationships that grow over time and others that wither. In all of these days, you can turn to God with gratitude, acknowledgement, or requests.

This section of prayers and the variation in their tone and style is meant to represent the range of energies you may carry into your classroom. While the Blessings for Seasons are about the occasions themselves, these prayers focus on the teacher's presence, her very being, in the midst of what is happening inside and outside the life of the school. I hope these prayers help you embrace the constant renewal of your heart and mind.

The Lord bless you and keep you,
Sheila

P.S. Some of these prayers are not inspired by my own life story, so I have taken steps to collect memories, thoughts, and feelings from teachers close to me who have experienced these situations.

Prayers for Entering the Classroom

Every Day

God, give me energy enough for this day. Fill me with love that overflows. May my work glorify you.
Amen.

Before the First Day

Their names are
on my roll.
I have seen
their data,
already been
flooded with
stats and scores.

This year, Lord,
let me see
their souls.
Amen.

On the First Day of School

I praise you, God, for new
beginnings.

The pencils are long,
the erasers intact.
Our folders are clean,
our paper crisp.
All that we need
is here.

Lockers,
desks,
and cubbies
are assigned and labeled,
but the question
on the heart
of each student
is whether she
will belong.

We will cross the threshold
from television, summer camps,
   and vacations
into shared space
and work.

We may enter
with excitement,
nervousness,
or even tears.
Some children will come eagerly
while others will need a nudge,
preferring the freedom
of their summer routine.

Bind us together
as we learn
to live in community.
I pray that the joy of today
fuels celebrations all year,
that our storehouse of patience
outlasts our frustrations,
and that our love only grows
in proportion to weariness.

We are refreshed and ready.
Let the excitement of this day
be our energy
through the year.
Amen.

My First Year

I appeal to you, Rabbi, as I enter my first classroom.
My students, *my students*, will enter this space today.
I beg your presence here.
Every morning of this year will be an act of humility,
a daily confession that I need You.

I have prepared, but I could never be ready.
It's impossible to predict what this day might hold
while looking at empty seats and a class roster.
There is surely more I could have done,
perhaps should have done,
but time has run out.

I still have so much to learn;
reveal to me mentors who are wise.
There will be struggles and celebrations;
give me friends to share the journey.
I will make mistakes and missteps;
provide leaders to keep me on course.

Cast out my fear so that I can shine a light that glorifies you.
Amen.

After Many Years

It is not my first year in this classroom, Lord, but it is theirs.

Repetition threatens to dull my senses. Remove the illusion of sameness and restore the wonder to my ordinary days. The spirit of futility invites bitterness into my heart. Open my eyes to Christ's presence in each small victory. Grant me the excitement of novelty and the poise of experience.
Amen.

My Last Year

God of the seasons who created a time for everything,
My days of teaching are coming to end.
Thank you for the years of possibility.

Thank you for the students and parents
who have shared their lives with me,
for those who expressed gratitude
and the ones who never returned.

Thank you for the teachers and administrators
who mentored me through every season,
guarding me from the naivety of youth
and the cynicism of experience.
Thank you for the challenges that have refined me,
the conflicts that have defined me,
and the celebrations that have sustained me
throughout the years of my teaching career.

Give me strength to finish the race
and bring glory to your name.
Help me show up fully each day
so that my lessons are relevant,
my materials are fresh,
and my outlook is optimistic.
Reveal opportunities to serve the next generation,
using my seniority to create space for others.
Amen.

AFTER MATERNITY LEAVE

Divine Father and Mother in one,
Thank you for the sweet days
    consumed
with meeting the needs of my baby.
Milk, diapers, laundry, and naps
    on an endless loop.
Her cry has been my alarm clock;
her wellbeing has been my agenda.
Surrounded by soft blankets
    and soothing music,
I've had hours each day to study
    her face,
hear her voice, and feel her breath
    on my skin.

After months of pregnancy
and weeks of feeding her,
I hardly know my own body.
Skin stretched and marked,
tissue swelling and contracting.
Latent miracles hidden in my flesh
since the day you formed Eve.
I am aware of the new fit of
    my clothes
and the scents of mothering
that linger on the fabric.

I confess my distractedness
as I enter my classroom.
I cannot remember
my last
full night
of sleep.
My mind is clouded
so that the simplest thoughts
remain
just out of reach.

I've been out so long
and missed so much.
I am overwhelmed by the thought
of sharing space
with my students again.
Constant movement,
countless decisions,
a cacophony of announcements,
questions,
and demands.

God, help me be present for my
    students.
May their greetings give me energy,
their questions endear them to me,
and our day together remind me
that you have provided meaningful
    work
in many forms.
Amen.

In a New Grade Level

I come to you humbly, Lord, asking for your presence in a new grade level. My previous year may not have been easy, but it was familiar. I knew what to expect of the students, the curriculum, and my colleagues. Now I am entering a new land.

I will not be as familiar with the levels my students are on. Help me identify and communicate the expectations and boundaries they need.

I will join a team, bringing my personality and values to the collective dynamic. We will negotiate how we do work, how we do conflict, and how we celebrate. I pray for peace among us.

Remind me to be patient; there are things I cannot know until I have lived in this cycle for a year. Be with me, Lord.
Amen.

At a New Campus

God, I have taken a path of change, and I feel as awkward, nervous, and excited as any student ever has. I've considered what to wear and even which water bottle might make the best impression with my new colleagues and students.

I don't yet know the routines and procedures that will be my lifeline in this place. Show me the people who can answer my many questions. Help me learn quickly which reports are due and to whom. Show me the tasks that are held in high regard and the ones that are better done than perfect.

Open my mind and heart to this new community. Steer me from gossip and divisive talk. Help me to see people as you would, not as hearsay might portray them. Give me a group of colleagues that I can share the joy and challenges of our work with, who will make me grow.
Amen.

When I Have a Student Teacher

I am entering my classroom in a different role while I have a student teacher, but my job is the same. I am here to teach.

The lessons that she learns from me will not only be what I prepared ahead of time but also the unscripted moments of discipline and decision-making. She will hear how I speak to and speak about my colleagues, my students, and their families. I pray that she sees evidence of your Spirit come from me, whether in the teacher's lounge, during recess, or on the Internet.

For her to learn, I will need to release control. It's not easy for me, Lord. Teach me when to step in and when to keep silent. When I speak, let me do so with a spirit of generosity, for the sake of good teaching, not the sake of my ego.

Give me a spirit of abundance, so that I'm glad to share not only the lessons I've learned, but also my files, my supplies, and my time. When my students bring her tokens of their affection, I want to celebrate, not covet, their regard for her.

I need a willingness to learn from her and the resources she has at her disposal, not the least of which may be an optimistic spirit, not yet worn down by the system. I pray that the fresh perspective she brings from her education will infuse new energy into my classroom. Give me the humility to applaud when her ideas yield better results than mine. *Amen.*

After a Conflict at Home

God, I call to you.

My mind is not on teaching. It is occupied with replaying the fight we had. I still hear the words we each spoke and the things left unspoken, what I wish I'd said and what I'd like to take back. I relive the emotions, feeling anxious, angry, heartbroken, and back again. I am exhausted, Lord.

I want to hide away, to bury my face in a pillow and pull blankets over my head. I want to stomp and scream and cry. Clear my heart, Lord. Do not let the dissension in my home spill over into my class. For now, I am preparing to share this space with my students.

They will not know what I have experienced or what I am still experiencing in my heart and mind. They will bring me questions about homework, stories of their pets, and bizarre treasures they found on the way into the building. Help me carry on.

My students demand so much, and I have committed to meeting them here. Help me be fully present and able to love them. Protect them from misdirected frustration. Give me the patience I need to walk beside them, in close contact with all of their little irritations. Help me choose patience. Remind me that they are not to blame.

Teach me to forgive and to ask forgiveness.
Amen.

After Divorce

In these early days when the fracture is fresh, Lord, carry me through. Grant me the wholeness to be available to my students and colleagues. Give me the energy to do my job, completely and well.

Today, I enter my classroom carrying my grief and distraction, yet something more abides along the edges. You have planted seeds for my future, and you are faithful to redeem every circumstance of my life. Reveal your love to me. *Amen.*

When Life at Home is Hard

Lord, life at home is full of challenges, and the anxiety follows me to work. It consumes my thoughts and drains my energy. There is little time in my day to use the bathroom, much less regroup when I cannot hold myself together.

I beg you to hem me in, Lord, both behind and before. Lay your hand on me. Provide what I need for this day. Grant me joy in my students, meaning in my work, and comfort in this space. *Amen.*

While Grieving

My heart is heavy with the weight of grief. My eyes look out at my classroom, but they hardly take in the scene. In the circle of those who have shared my grief, I can speak of ordinary things. We've spent our tears together and found ourselves on the other side.

Here, I feel like a stranger in a strange place. When they ask how I am doing, I feel the tears burn as though a new well has sprung. Sometimes they don't ask, and it is both a mercy and an affront. How can they be so casual when nothing will be ordinary again?

I will rejoin my students today. They will be ordinary. Their attention will drift, their pencils will break, and they will surprise me with both kindness and carelessness. Lift the veil of grief for these hours so that I can see them. May I revel in their ordinariness.

Have mercy on me, Lord. Thank you for these reminders of life. *Amen.*

When I Am Tired
I need you, Lord. Be near me and sustain me.

Today is one of those days when the alarm came too early. My mind is in a fog, and I'm moving mechanically through our routines.

Guard me from crankiness and impatience. Protect my students from my own weariness so that my exhaustion doesn't become a weapon used against them.

Sharpen my mind. Focus my thoughts on the importance of my job and my reasons for showing up. Give me energy to do my work well.
Amen.

When I Don't Feel Well
Lord, have mercy on me today. I don't feel well, but it is easier to be here than to be gone.

I pray that my students will be cooperative and that the work I've put into establishing routines, preparing lessons, and organizing materials will pay off. Minimize the need for redirection.

Give me strength for today and healing for tomorrow.
Amen.

When I have Morning Sickness
Father, thank you for the miracle that grows within me. Even as I recognize the gift of new life, I groan with the sickness that comes with it. There are moments when I am overcome.

You can calm the sea, Lord; please still my churning stomach. Protect me from strong scents and sudden movements. Provide opportunities for snacking, and watch over my students when I must leave them.
Amen.

When All is Good

God, you have brought me through seasons of trial and into this time of blessing when I am well and whole. Out of your goodness, reveal to me ways that I can serve my students and colleagues. Let me be a light to those in darkness and a friend to those who are lonely.
Amen.

When I'm Worried

Lord, forgive me.

I have entered my classroom with worry.

I have allowed my mind to race, imagining scenes that may never come to pass. I have given the enemy space in my heart, and he has planted false images of failure and hopelessness.

Train my mind to see what is good and true. Let me trust in your promises, confident that I can do all things when I lean on your strength and not my own.

Lord, remind me to lay my worries down. May my work be for your glory rather than an attempt to prove my worth. I am enough because you called me and your grace is sufficient. Today, I will take comfort knowing that you will provide everything I need.
Amen.

WHEN I'M AFRAID

Lord, I am struggling to enter my classroom. The enemy prowls, and fear is the greatest threat.

I am afraid that my students will not like me, connect with me, or find me relevant. I am afraid they will not respond to my attempts at order. If they are out of control, disrespectful, or just plain mean, I will be powerless to stop them.

I even find myself scared of their parents. Most are patient, gracious, and kind, so I fear letting them down. A few are spiteful and seem set on my defeat. I fear their anger and retribution.

I fear my students will ask a question I can't answer. I will be exposed as a fraud, and my imperfections will be exploited.

I'm afraid a test given to my students will prove my own incompetence. My methods will be questioned, my efforts will be proven worthless, and my shame will be public.

Fear tempts me to retreat, but isolation makes me easy prey. Connect me to community, and fill me with perfect love to drive out fear. *Amen.*

ON MY BIRTHDAY

Jesus, thank you for the celebration of another year. Though some people take days off or experience wild adventures, I have chosen to enter my classroom on my special day.

After all, it's not everyone who has their birthday announced over a loudspeaker or enjoys a serenade of young voices.

I can anticipate sweet cards, written in haste, even from students who I didn't know cared, and a special treat from a coworker.

It will also be a day of work. You have blessed my life with work, and through work my days have life. I have lessons to teach, meetings to attend, and tasks to complete, and in doing these things, I will celebrate.
Amen.

When There's Nowhere I'd Rather Be
Lord, it is good for me to be here! I am overcome with gratitude.

Thank you for the work you've set before me. It is meaningful, rich, and life-giving. Thank you for the students who join me every day. They challenge me in ways that awaken my spirit. Thank you for my colleagues that share in this work. They celebrate me in success and sustain me in defeat. Thank you for the challenges I will face today and the opportunities they provide to learn and grow.

May I live today in the light of your love and may the joy you have given me shine a light for others and bring glory to your name.
Amen.

With Mindfulness
Lord,

Keep me mindful of the most important thing:
to be excellent in teaching
so that my students
have greater opportunities.
Keep me mindful of the little things, too.
Attendance and lunch count
are big things
in another person's day.
Amen.

In Conflict with a Colleague

Examine my heart, Lord. I am not at peace with my colleague.

As I enter my classroom today, Lord, search my heart and remove that which is not from you. Replace envy, bitterness, and begrudging with patience, peace, and gentleness. Give me the courage and the opportunity to approach her with honesty and grace. Teach me to forgive and to humbly ask forgiveness. Set my mind on teaching and serving my students. Allow me to throw off the resentment that ensnares me so that I can complete the tasks you've set before me. Amen.

After a Difficult Meeting

Lord, there are times when I want to retreat, but I must enter my classroom. The meeting was difficult. Emotions were high and conflicting, and I am left exhausted. My mind needs time to process the conversation and its outcomes, both positive and negative. I need to consider the next steps. I want to replay the words I heard and the ones I spoke.

Instead, I am returning to my classroom as though all is well. Give me breath, Lord. Let me inhale the peace that only comes from you and my identity as your child. Let me exhale the anxiety that threatens to take root.

Focus my mind on the tasks you've blessed me with at this time, on this day. I will greet my students, and we will carry on. I will teach and engage wholeheartedly, despite the fractures that threaten to bring me down and shut them out.

Grant me the courage and the will to answer your calling to teach. Amen.

After an Attack on a School
Lord of light, enter this world of darkness.

I cannot see the images on the screen without imagining my own students being escorted by policemen out of a building, down the street, and to a "safe place" where parents wait. I cannot see the faces of anguish or relief without thinking of the parents who delivered their children to our building on the first day of school. I think of the students in my class now and in previous years, doing quick math to figure out which group would be the age of the most recent victims.

School was supposed to be their safe place. As I enter my classroom today, I can't help but wonder how secure our building really is. Despite our technology, precautions, and drills, I know too well that we are never far from evil while we live in this world. You've promised no earthly fortress, but, God, I beg you to protect the boundaries of this school. Keep us from those who would inflict violence on children.

As we enter the classroom, I will welcome my students into a space that should be safe, but some of them will have also realized that it might not be. We have seen too much to believe it anymore. Show me the way to provide comfort to those who are scared. In a world of violence and fear, Lord, make me a vessel of peace.
Amen.

WHEN SCHOOLS ARE IN THE SPOTLIGHT
God,

The news cycle has brought us under scrutiny, and their reports have everyone talking. They don't ask about me, or my students, or the actual things we do day in and day out, but the undefined "school system" and "teachers," of collective imagination.

The spotlight shines on vague entities, but the glare impairs my vision. Everything reported is not accurate, and everything reported is not wrong. Everyone has an opinion, but I have a job to do.

Refine my focus, clear my path, and set my heart on what is true.
Amen.

AFTER A DIFFICULT PARENT CONFERENCE
Lord, you've given me satisfaction in the challenge of teaching my students, but working with their parents can sometimes bend me low. I do my best to prepare for our meetings, but today I am undone. The swell of emotions and the energy spent keeping the surge in check have left me exhausted in mind, body, and spirit.

I will need to process the meeting. I will need to unpack all that was said and decided. For now, though, it is time to return to my classroom and to teaching. Help me focus my thoughts and energy on my students and their needs. Clear my heart so that I can be present for them.
Amen.

NEAR A HOLIDAY
Thank you, Lord, for giving us hearts that celebrate, and the times set aside in our year to do so.

I come before you today acknowledging that while these days are full of fun, they are also exhausting. My mind is prone to wander even as I need to be at my best.

Lord, give me patience. Let me see my students' hearts before their behaviors. We feed their energy with everything from bulletin boards to music, then flinch when their excitement overflows in outbursts that startle us both.

We all thrive within boundaries, so Lord, help me be diligent in communicating them, creating the structure that will keep us safe and productive. Grant me focus so that my own desire for a break doesn't become the catalyst for our folly.
Amen.

On a Rainy Day
Thank you, Lord, for the rain and the life it brings to earth. Thank you for giving us a dry place to gather.

As I begin my day, I pray that the sound of the rain be a reminder of the life you've poured over me, as I become ever aware of your blessings. My heart is full of thanks for all that you provide.
As the rain falls outside, set our minds on the work before us.

As we go through transitions, help my students resist the temptation of puddles. They are overcome by impulse, not considering the discomfort of hours in wet clothes.

Rainy days affect us in different ways. May those with excess energy bring life to our learning. May those overcome by sleepiness bring calm. May we all find focus.

At the end of this day, watch over our dismissal. Keep us safe as we leave this place.
Amen.

On the First Snowy Day

It is cold and wet outside, but we find warmth and welcome as we enter this place. Thank you for the shelter you've given us. I thank you that children who may not have heat at home can find warmth in these hours.

Thank you for the wonder of snow. Children are drawn by your splendor, pointing at windows with wide-eyed excitement. I am compelled to join them, standing in awe at the work of your hands.

As the snow lays a quiet blanket over the world outside, anticipation bubbles over in our classroom. Some will want to throw up their hands and run headlong into the flurry, impervious to its chill. Others daydream of a cozy spot buried under blankets. It is easy to forget that we have come together for a purpose.

And there, Lord, is the tension. We have come to this place to teach and to learn. Be with us today as we live with competing desires. Teach me to recognize the moments you've given us to marvel at your creation. Then energize my heart for teaching, so that I can engage my students with what I have planned. Give my students curiosity that rivals their wonder for the phenomenon outside the window. Help us focus on the tasks before us, even as our imaginations create pictures of what we would rather be doing.
Amen.

The Last Day of School

I praise you, God, for bringing us to the finish line.

No one can find a pencil longer than a pinkie finger. Crayons are broken, markers are dry, and the corners of every folder are bent, perhaps chewed. Labels carefully applied to desks and lockers have disappeared, leaving sticky residue in their place. We are worn out as well.

You have carried us so far, Lord. The newness has worn off, but in its place is a community. We have lived many hours together, learning, growing, and sometimes struggling. We've accumulated inside jokes and even developed our own culture based on months of shared experiences. We've been frustrated and hurt by each other, and we've learned to be patient and to forgive. We've celebrated and loved each other well.

Now we will cross the threshold from backpacks and bell schedules into new rhythms apart from each other. We will spend our days in front of the television, at summer jobs, or on vacation. Some will be eager to leave while others will need a nudge, preferring the familiarity of our classroom routine. Our goodbyes will be filled with excitement and nervousness and perhaps a few tears. We are weary and ready.

Bless us and keep us, Lord.
Amen.

PRAYERS FOR

The Community

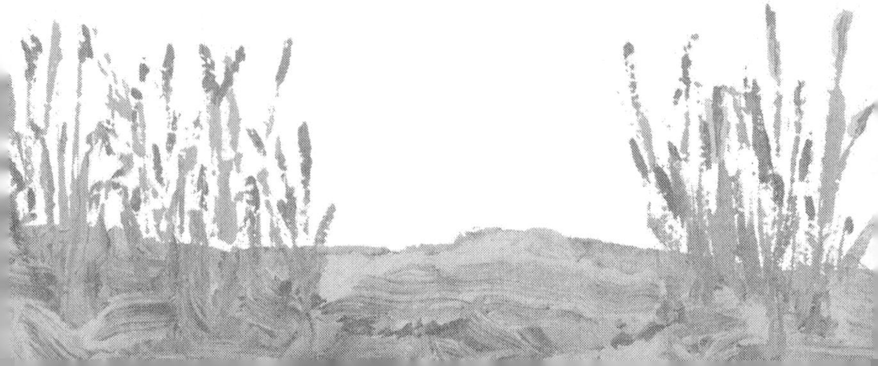

INTRODUCTION TO

Prayers for the Community

Dear Teacher,

*E*arly in my teaching career, I was proud to tell strangers on airplanes or at social events that I was a teacher. Then I learned that many people heard that as an invitation to explain to me how easily the education system could be fixed if *only*. They would point a confident finger at the teachers, the students, their parents, the school board, or the media. Aside from being grossly reductive, their solutions seemed bent on pitting the members of the school community against each other.

In contrast, this section of prayers aims for empathy and unity. Paul says about the church that "we are one body with many parts."[4] Similarly, the education of children doesn't happen only in my classroom. There are the classrooms down the hallway, school boards who make decisions, families who partner with us, and even the critics who challenge us to be better. Parker Palmer observed that division is in the air we breathe, so students "have been taught to cope with the collapse of community but never challenged by a vision of community renewed."[5] We should not be at odds with each other. Rather, we should be unified and accountable to one another.

The prayers in this section cover an intentionally broad community. In the same way that Jesus challenged his listeners to broaden their understanding of *neighbor*, this section encourages you to pray for a wide-ranging community. Not only does that include those who support you, but also those you may not have noticed in the background of your day, as well as those who oppose your work or threaten the well-being of your students. I'm moved by Palmer's assertion that "in God's hospitality we learn that close, warm, and enduring relations are not the only ones which enrich our lives. Indeed, we may learn less about ourselves in those relations than in more distant, occasional, and even abrasive ones."[5]

While there is overlap between this section and others, these prayers are distinct in their being *for* others. The laments may be about others, but these are meant to be blessings *for* them. The Bible tells us that in Christ all things hold together and that Christ is making peace.[6] My hope is that over time these prayers create space for you to imagine *your* community held together and living in peace.

The Lord bless you and keep you,
Sheila

Prayers for the Community

For the Ones Who Make Decisions
Bless those who make decisions for our schools.
They are appointed, elected, and paid,
but rarely are they teachers.
Give them eyes to see the work we do,
wisdom to recognize its importance,
courage to bear witness,
and fortitude to bolster our efforts.
Amen.

For the Custodial Staff
God, thank you for the ones who keep our building clean. They are an essential part of the work we do, yet their days are often thankless. Forgive me when I do not see them.
When a student gets sick, we may clear the room, but our custodial staff enters. When a toilet overflows and a sign tells everyone to stay out, they go in. They vacuum leaves in the fall, salt sidewalks in the winter, mop footprints in the spring, and move furniture in the summer.

God, place it on our hearts and on our systems to provide for them financially. My students are watching, learning from me how to treat those who are not in positions of power. Lord, show me the way.
Amen.

For the School Administrators

To the God of Moses, Joshua, Esther, and Deborah,
bless those who lead us.

Give them wisdom to do what is best
in the moment and for the time to come.

Increase their courage and stamina
to follow through with their intentions.

Let them lead with confidence,
leaning on the assurance of your goodness and grace.

May they hold their power loosely,
as a responsibility you have given rather than a prize they've earned.

Grant them time to do their work.
Hold back the tide of distractions, demands, and fear.

Protect their hearts from dismay
when the tasks seem too large, the lists too long, and the complaints too loud.

Bring them out of isolation and toward community,
as you reveal friends who can walk beside them on their journey.
Amen.

For the Office Staff

Dear God, thank you for those who work in the office,
managing our systems and our days.
I don't know how they do their work between
accepting deliveries of supplies and forgotten lunch boxes;
fielding questions about schedules, menus, and policies;
monitoring children who wait for parents, the principal, and the nurse;
and collecting stories from everyone who passes through.

Bless them as they offer hospitality to all who come, on the phone and in person. Give them the fortitude to hear so much yet maintain confidentiality, even when such knowledge could be traded for personal gain. May they greet the well-to-do and the not-doing-well with equal grace. Sustain them in times of stress, and strengthen them for the trouble that others bring their way.

Provide a salary that recognizes the essential nature of the work they do, and bless their families just as they bless us.
Amen.

For the Cafeteria Staff
Lord, bless the hands that prepare food for so many. They begin their work early in the morning, in anticipation of the students who count on them for breakfast and lunch each day. They work with a tight budget to transform bulk bags of frozen food into hundreds of hot meals. They keep accounts yet show no preference for the wealthy or the poor standing in their lines. All who are hungry are invited to eat.

They stand before streams of children, grateful or grumbling, and serve them all. They know the children by name and even remember who will prefer a hotdog to a hamburger. How many children? How many reminders that they must choose a vegetable and that rolls are not vegetables? How many slices of pizza with a side of corn? How many insults about the food they've worked hard to prepare?

I am guilty of rushing out, anxious to leave my students in the care of someone else, not taking the time to say thank you. I confess that I have regarded myself more highly than them, my time more valuable, or my contribution more essential. Forgive my arrogance, Lord.
Amen.

For the Counselor Who Tends to Children's Hearts

Our school exists for the purpose of teaching and learning, but our students need much more than academics. Bless our school counselor. She spends her days in the presence of children who need more than our classrooms can offer. She sits with them in their darkest times and teaches them the skills to thrive. She holds their vulnerability with gentleness and provides a safe place for them to be honest about their experiences in the world.

Bless her words that they may be truthful and kind.
Bless her silence that it may create space for healing and growth.
Bless her spirit that she may enter each conversation wholeheartedly.
Give her wisdom, truth, and persistence.
Comfort her with your peace.
Amen.

For the Counselor Who Coordinates Schedules and Testing

God, bless our counselor who coordinates schedules and testing. Her days are deep in details, putting together a puzzle even as the pieces change shape. She is bound by rules, constraints, and deadlines outside of her control even as she is tasked with implementation that fits our campus needs.

Her job is often thankless. When her work keeps everything running smoothly, it goes unnoticed, as though order from chaos was a small thing. When her work inconveniences us, she surely hears about it. When we do not like the message she delivers or the restrictions she holds us to, we bring our frustration to her.

Lord, reveal to her, and to us, the role our counselor plays in the goals we are all working toward. Give her space, both mental and physical, to work without interruption. Prepare us to feel empathy and to give her grace as she extends the same to us.
Amen.

For the School Nurse
Lord, I humbly ask You to bless our school nurse.

Bless her persistence
as she cleans and disinfects to prevent the spread of disease.

Bless her hands
as she dispenses medication, checks temperatures, and applies bandages.

Bless her mind
as she considers the students' needs and makes a plan for care.

Bless her words
as she completes paperwork and communicates with parents.

Bless her healing work
as she comforts the sick, aching, heartbroken, and tired.

Bless her heart
when the best treatment is a kind word given with a peppermint, a saltine cracker, or a drink of water.

Bless her spirit
when she cannot heal the child's wounds.
Amen.

For the Instructional Coaches
God,

Bless our instructional coaches. They are here to support us, though at times we find ourselves at odds. Deepen our relationships. Show us the beauty in our differences and the power in our unity.

Give them a spirit of curiosity, entering our classrooms with questions, not accusations or advice. May they assume that we are doing the best we can on this day, at this time. I pray they listen to understand then draw out our wisdom and experience before showcasing their own. Prepare the way for us to meet productively. May each gathering have a clear, vital purpose so that we can all speak plainly, guided by mutual trust and common goals.

Evidence of the coaches' success can be elusive since action must come from the classrooms and accountability from the office. Give them self-assurance as they hold up standards and provide support. Make their role clear so that their job is not reduced to gossip-girl, tattletale, or middleman. When tasks are assigned that are outside the scope of their responsibilities, give them the discernment to know when to draw a boundary. Clear a path for them to do the work they were meant to do, rather than the work no one else wants.
Amen.

For Our Faculty
God, bless this faculty. Though we spend most hours isolated from each other, there is no one who knows what I do better than the other teachers on this campus. Teach us to love each other well. Remove the gossip, comparisons, and petty judgments that would do us harm.

We are many individuals, united by a common purpose.
We are a collective, containing many unique perspectives.
Teach us the beauty of belonging, even as we nurture our distinctiveness.
Amen.

For My Team
From the beginning, Lord, you gave us work to do and recognized that we could not do it well alone. As I undertake a job that is often done behind closed doors, I am especially thankful for my team.

They are my sounding board and thinking partners. We share the burden of planning and preparing the lessons that we will carry out individually, and I am mindful that they shape my attitudes and beliefs.
Grant us wisdom and awareness of the ways we influence each other.

When we are together, I pray that we will be united in our best intentions. Show us how to create space for creativity and risk-taking. Make it a safe place for honesty in the pursuit of improvement. In our times together, let us grow in our skills and our spirits.
Give us the courage to make each other better.

I pray that professionalism guides us, not in the service of workplace compliance, but in answer to your call to be set apart from those who would gossip, deceive, or do harm. Keep us from distractions that darken our hearts and disrupt our work.
Give us peace to work as a team.

Bless my colleagues when they leave this place.
May their work provide for their homes and may their homes support their work.
Amen.

For the Colleague I Dislike

God of all goodness,
you tell me to love my enemy,
to pray for her and not to
    curse her.

The enemy is near.

Lord, I come to you humbly
to pray for my colleague.
Bless her coming and going,
her work, and her rest.
Amen.

For the Colleague Who is Struggling

Father, I pray to you on behalf of
    my colleague.
Shine your light in her darkness.
Heal the wounds that bind her,
take up the burdens that she
    bears, and
give her a friend in times
    of loneliness.
Reveal the depths of your mercy.
Amen.

For the Colleague I Depend On

God, you know my heart and you see my needs before I do. Thank you for putting ____ in my life. She understands more than anyone the struggles and successes that shape my waking hours.

She is the one whose classroom I can pop my head into and with nothing more than a look, she understands that something funny, disheartening, or wonderful has happened. She knows why I laugh and understands when the laughter turns to tears.

She can tell, without my saying, which days are hard. When I am low, she stays beside me until the storm has passed. She understands the importance of a Sonic run, the comfort of good coffee, and the power of chocolate. Her voice cheers me, and her words renew my spirit. I know that I am richly blessed.

When my lessons grow stale and the standards elusive, when I've exhausted my strategies for helping a student or approaching a parent, I can go to her. She knows when to listen and when to speak. She asks the questions that open my mind to new possibilities. Her strengths complement my weaknesses.

We have walked through the professional gauntlet and become stronger together. I admit there are days when I am overwhelmed by the demands placed before me, but you have given me this friend, and I can endure.

Be near to my dear colleague, Lord. May she be blessed with the full measure of goodness she has given to me.
Amen.

For the Substitute Teacher

Lord bless the substitute teacher. Thank you for bringing her to our campus and to my classroom. Fill her with a spirit of confidence and authority, tempered with a heart of kindness. May her words be firm, but never mean. Give her energy and persistence to make it through the day.

I pray that she is on time, well rested, and prepared for the work she's taken on. Lord, I pray that she is able to find everything she needs: the plans and materials I prepared, the adult restroom, and money for the vending machine.

Lord, I beg that she follows my plans regardless of her feelings about them. Raise a helper from the sea of faces before her. Give her the wisdom and humility to follow the guidance of my trusted students and nearby colleagues.

It is a difficult job that often goes without thanks; may she know the gratitude I feel.
Amen.

For the Student Teacher

Thank you for a new generation of teachers. Bless the student who will soon be my colleague. Give her endurance as the days grow long, the new wears off, and the adrenaline is gone. Care for her when the financial burden of work without pay takes its toll.

Give her humility. Teach her to listen, ask questions, and then continue listening. Show her when to defer to my instruction, making the most of our time together. Reveal to her the insight of mentors. May she recognize the value of experience and the collective wisdom that comes from years of practice.

Give her confidence. Let criticism based on age and assumptions roll off her back. Let her stand tall in front of the students who will challenge her not because of any fault, but because it is in their nature. Lift up her voice when she has an idea to contribute. May she recognize the value of her education and the fresh perspective she brings to our work.
Amen.

For My Class

Lord, I ask your blessing on my class, these children that I call "mine" for a year.

Thank you for the diversity among us. Each unique story brings richness to the whole. Lord, allow them to grow under my guidance and in spite of it when necessary.

Soften my heart to those I love but find harder to like. Give me eyes to see your likeness in each of them.

For the ones who find learning easy, I pray they develop humility. Show me ways to challenge them so that they experience the satisfaction of hard work.

For the ones who struggle, I pray they develop persistence. Show me how to teach in ways they can understand so that they experience the sweetness of accomplishment.
Amen.

For My Class When I Am Absent
Father, dwell in my class while I am gone.

Most of the students will simply go through the routine of another day. Expand their influence in the class.

Others will consider my absence an opportunity to create disruption. Place a restraint on their wills.

For a few, I am the most consistent factor in their lives.
Give them peace in my absence.

Some will be eager to help, to be of use, to demonstrate how much
    they know.
Teach them to speak when it is helpful and to remain quiet when it's not.

Lord, bless the attention-seekers, the worriers, the helpers,
    and the onlookers.
Keep them safe until I return.
Amen.

FOR A STUDENT ON HER BIRTHDAY
Lord, I pray a special blessing on ____ today.
Thank you for the years she has lived.
Watch over her as she begins a new one.
May her ears hear the truth of your promises,
may her feet lead her down paths of righteousness,
may her eyes see the wonder of your love,
and may her life bring glory to your name.
Amen.

FOR A STUDENT WHO IS SICK
Lord, bless ____ while she is sick and away from our class.

Provide comfort to her body. In her comfort, let her rest. And in resting, let her heal. Guard her heart and mind as she seeks diversion from boredom.

Bless her caregivers and allow them to be with her without worry for financial retribution. Provide them the means to seek medical expertise and medications when necessary.

Bring her back to us soon, fully recovered.
Amen.

For a New Student
Thank you for bringing a new student into our community.

When she is anxious, show me what she needs to feel safe. Give her courage to try new things and to ask questions. Guard her heart with your spirit of peace.

When she is lonely, raise up a friend who will welcome her into our routines and relationships. Let her hold dear the memories of her former school, friends, and learning.

When she is unsure, give her boldness. Prepare her heart to welcome the new blessings you have in store for her.
Amen.

For a Student Who Is Moving
Dear God,
When a member of our classroom family leaves, we all experience the loss. Bless ____'s departure from us.

I pray that you place people and experiences before her that will help her grow and learn. Keep her safe from harm. Give her new friends and adults she can depend on.

May the time we've shared on our journeys be a blessing to her as our paths take new directions. Lord, bless her and keep her on the road ahead.
Amen.

For the Student Whose Parents Are Struggling

Lord, bless this child who wears her shirt from yesterday and the day before. She goes through the motions of turning in her folder, while we both know that there are no signatures and her homework is not complete. No adult is available for this child at home.

Assure her that she is loved. Let her recognize your word on her heart and know that she is not alone. Give her a spirit of peace in a world that is chaotic.

While her parents are struggling, surround her with safety in the form of other adults, friends, and caregivers. Protect her in this time of uncertainty.

God, I know she never escapes your notice. Protect her from those who would see her weakness as an opportunity to do her harm. Lead her not into temptation. Keep the wolves away from this precious lamb.

Thank you for the resilience that you bless children with.
Amen.

For a Bully

Lord, my heart cries out for justice. Even though she is a child, she is hurtful to the other children that I love. She weaponizes her strengths and threatens the wellbeing of her classmates.

You are the God of justice. You hear the cry of the underdog, and you are never silent forever. Bring your justice. Show me what I should do.

Lord, my heart cries out for mercy. Despite her behavior, she is also a child that I love. I have no doubt that she has been hurt, even if I cannot see her wounds. She is trying to protect herself from further injury.

You are the God of mercy. You hear the cry of the broken spirit, and you are moved. Heal your wounded child. Show me what I should do.
Amen.

FOR A STUDENT WHO IS BULLIED

Lord, have mercy on the child who is bullied.
Heal her body and her spirit, too.
Amid insults and injury,
when she is tempted to believe that she is not enough,
assure her that she was wonderfully made.
Protect her spirit from despair
and her heart from bitterness.
Remind her of the promises you've spoken.
May the assurance of her worth
give her courage to speak up.
Give her words to say
and the confidence to set firm boundaries.
When retreat is the only solution,
reveal the path to safety.
Place adults in her life who will listen
and believe her story.
Give her safe places and communities
to be at ease in her own skin.
Send a friend to this child.
Amen.

For the Marginalized

There are those among us
who have never been
allowed to fit in.

They stand on the edges,
gleaning what they can
from the rich man's fields.

You have always been
the God of the outcast.
Be their redeemer
in this place.

You say that
in your kingdom
the poor will be blessed,
the outcast will be embraced,
and the last will be first.

Give me compassion
to see their need,
hospitality
to welcome them,
and resolve
to clear their path.
Thy kingdom come, thy will be done
On earth as it is in heaven.
Amen.

For the English Language Learner

Oh Lord, I lift up my student whose first language is not English. Her days may feel overwhelming. I pray protection on the child's first language and all of the ways that it embodies her culture. May she continue to value it and not cast it aside.

Clear the path for her to learn. As she begins, I pray that hospitality is communicated with smiles and kind gestures. Provide space for her silence and bring her friends who will help her navigate the unknown.

Let her join quickly in the games of the playground, the laugher of the lunch table, and the chatter of the classroom. I pray that we will all appreciate the value inherent in our differences.

As she continues the journey toward academic achievement, give her endurance. Surround her with teachers and family members who will encourage her effort and be patient in her progress.

Above all, let this child encounter grace and beauty as she engages a new culture and its language.
Amen.

FOR THE CHILD WHO IS ABUSED
Lord, have mercy on this child. She is broken in body and spirit. I do not know how long she has endured abuse, but I know it is in her life today, so I lift ____'s name to you. You are the champion of the oppressed, and God, she needs an advocate. Place your protection around her.

Guard her body. Surround her with people of courage and strength; do not leave her vulnerable to abuse. Remove her from danger.

Guard her heart. Do not let the poison of abuse take root. Do not let the despair of victimhood become her identity or the perpetuation of abuse become her destiny. Remind her that she is your beloved child.

Walk beside her and make your presence known as she enters the flawed system put in place to protect her; it is a human system after all. May her dignity, privacy, and community be honored. May she find consolation in the knowledge that so many people are working on her behalf.
Amen.

For Parents Who are Abusive

Lord, I am angry. My student has been injured at the hands of the adults she should be able to trust. I come to you now on their behalf. Lord, reveal yourself to them with a blinding light. May they see in your goodness the redemption you offer to all. May they see in your righteousness that justice is in your hands. May they see in your patience how they ought to live.

Lord, have mercy.

They are your creation, yet they embody the brokenness that is in the world. Please heal the wounds of past abuse. Provide resources to alleviate the stress that leads them to lift a hand or voice to a child. Cast out the demons that haunt their thoughts so they can recognize the goodness you've written on their hearts. Remind them of who they were created to be. Instill a desire to break the pattern of abuse and give them a community who will support them on the road to restoration. *Amen.*

For the Family with Economic Needs

Lord of All,

I recognize the unwashed clothes and notice attempts to pocket extra food at breakfast. The lessons I teach are far from the child's mind. Her family is in need of your provision, Lord.

Bring comfort to their bodies and spirits. I pray that their needs will be met with compassion, not pity. Give them safe shelter with livable temperatures, food to eat, and water to drink and bathe in. Provide transportation that meets their needs for work and school. Make known to them the resources that will fill the gaps so that they can resume material care for their children. Increase their dignity and diminish their shame. *Amen.*

For the Parent Volunteers

God our Father, thank you for the parents who volunteer.
Both the reluctant and the prideful,
those with plenty of time and the ones who squeeze it in,
the generous hearts and the ones seeking to advance their own agendas.
Their time is a gift, regardless of their motivations.

Thank you for the folders stuffed and papers filed;
everything laminated, cut, and sorted;
the book fair, fall festival, and class parties.
Bless the work of their hands and the expenditure of their time.

Unite us on the ground we share:
the love of their children and a desire for their success.
May we all work together for this common good.
Amen.

For the Parents Who Can't Volunteer

God bless the parents who can't volunteer.
Those with other children, demanding jobs, or school-related baggage;
those without margins.

Give them peace; remove the guilt they may feel.
Protect their hearts from comparison when it comes to steal their joy.
Let them rest in the assurance that my care for their children does not
    depend on their service.
Reveal opportunities for them to join our community in other ways.
Amen.

For the Families at School Events

God, bless the families gathered here. Parents, grandparents, siblings, and friends have committed this time to support the children they love. I usually experience my students on their own, but now I see a glimpse of the fullness of their lives, and I am moved.

Bless their time here and their journeys home. *Lord, bless and keep them. Shine your face on them and give them peace.*
Amen.

For the Overextended Family

When homework is incomplete, messages go unreturned, and notes are unsigned, I am quick to judge. Teach me to extend grace when my first instinct is criticism. Help me recognize myself in their difficult days.

Bless this family in this season when work is long and each day demands more than its twenty-four hours allow. In the presence of children with endless needs, entrenched in a culture that expects picture-perfection, Lord, I call out for your help. Envelop this family in your spirit of grace. Assure them that they are enough. Invite them into stillness so that they may act with purpose.
Amen.

For the Family Experiencing Divorce

Lord of light, walk with this family through the darkness. They are each hurting, weighed down by collective and individual burdens.

Be with the parents. I pray that they will treat each other with dignity and honor their partners in parenting. Lead them to draw appropriate boundaries between what needs to be said, what should be kept silent, and what conversations should wait for a better time. Comfort each of them in their individual experiences of grief, anger, and regret. I pray that you fill them with civility and respect more than competition.

Cast out all pettiness, greed, and envy. Give them a love for their child that far outweighs her value as a bargaining chip. Protect them each financially so that they may both care for their child.

Be with this child. May she be surrounded with steadiness and consistency. May her schedule be predictable and manageable, and may she feel as little disruption as possible. Guard her from any harsh words spoken. Protect her from feelings of guilt or shame, and as she grows, cast out narratives that come from such lies. Surround her with loving adults who can provide security in this season of uncertainty. Give her answers to the questions that haunt her sleep. Comfort her in the dark, quiet moments.
Amen.

For the Critics

Lord, you know that teaching is hard. The job is only made more difficult by those who criticize, hurling insults and diminishing our work. I raise our critics to you in prayer. I am grateful for the concern people have for our children and for the future of our society. Thank you for their good intentions.

Open their eyes to the work we do. Let them see the sacrifices we make on behalf of the children in our community. Please introduce them to teachers who represent the best of our profession as a counter to the others who too often make headlines.

Reveal to them ways that they can get involved in our schools and spend their energy building us up rather than tearing us down. Quiet the volume and limit the spread of their divisive voices. Let the truth of their words cut through the noise of their tone. May they find helpful ways to voice their concerns.
Amen.

For My Family

Provider of all good things, I come to you with a prayer for my family.
Care for them and comfort them in my absence.
In my presence, Lord, let them see how much I love them.
In all times, let them see my heart for your kingdom.
Lord bless my children, who must share their mother with so many others.
Bless my partner who shares the physical and emotional toll of my work.
Nourish their bodies even when I prepare meals in haste, and nurture their spirits even when my body grows weak.
I pray your forgiveness and theirs when I do not recognize or meet their needs well.
Sustain them through the seasons of stress.
Help us create moments and seasons to restore our hearts and bring us closer together as we also draw close to you.
Amen.

For My Teachers
Dear God,

Thank you for all of my teachers. I have learned from many people in my life, but I maintain a special connection to those in the classroom.

Thank you for the best of these: the ones who loved me despite my imperfections, who recognized the best in me and called it out, who inspired curiosity and a desire to work harder, and who lived in integrity and wholeheartedness.

Thank you for the worst of these: the ones who taught me to endure hard years, whose voices persist as reminders of the long-term influence of a teacher's words, and who made me aware of the importance of integrity.

Thank you for the teachers who inspired me to teach: the ones who brought honor to the profession, whose practices were worthy of imitation, and who shaped my own identity as a teacher. I am still realizing the value of their expertise, presence, and passion.

Lord, bless them and keep them.
Amen.

PRAYERS OF

Lament

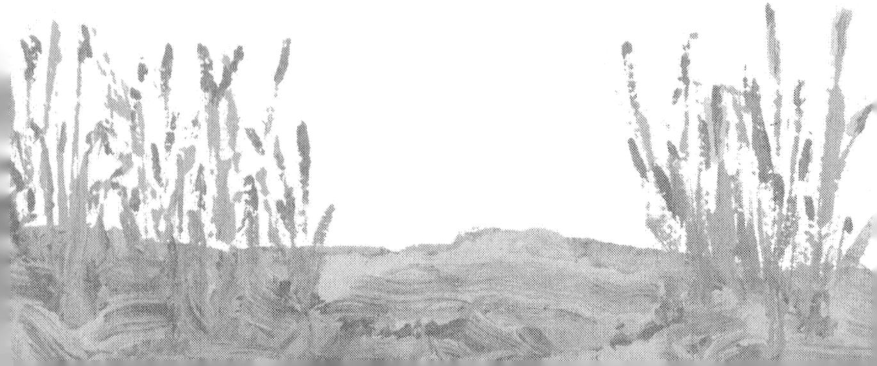

INTRODUCTION TO
Prayers of Lament

Dear Teacher,

I loved teaching. The time I spent in the classroom with my students energized me. I also enjoyed planning lessons, organizing my classroom, and working through problems. What didn't I love? Animosity between schools and families, low status and compensation, and unjust systems, to name a few things. Being a teacher doesn't always give you warm fuzzies inside.

Jealousy, frustration, loneliness, grief, and shame are normal parts of the teacher's inner terrain. Negative emotions, no matter how strong, are not signs that you are in the wrong profession. On the contrary, such strong feelings might indicate a level of care that is necessary for the job.

Our first inclination may be to ignore our negative feelings. We live in a culture that Barbara Brown Taylor calls "full solar spirituality"[7] in which we are encouraged to look on the bright side of everything. However, as Carl Jung observed, "How can I be substantial if I do not cast a shadow? I must have a dark side also if I am to be whole."[8]

A common response to our darker feelings is to try to handle them on our own. We use gossip to lay out our defenses and settle scores with those who have wronged us. We lash out in anger or frustration. We hide our fears behind verbal swords and shields, or we misuse our positions of power over students when we are faced with our own powerlessness.

In contrast to denial or manipulation, lament provides a healthy way to face our darkest moments. Lament requires both boldness and humility. Boldness is necessary to face the darkness head-on, to recognize it and name it. Humility is required to acknowledge your own frailty, then leave the vengeance, retribution, or rescue in God's hands. Inherent in lament is acknowledging that God is sovereign over all.

Prayers of lament are not uncontrolled rants. On the contrary, with structured movements of address, complaint, request, motivation, and confidence, lament is "a vocabulary to express the realities of our brokenness and a grammar that helps us control the vocabulary."[9] No matter how honest, a lament honors the holiness of God.

To make locating the lament you need easier, I have organized the section into categories of fear and worry, anger and frustration, grief and sadness, and confession. My hope is that these prayers give you the language you need to turn to God on your darkest days of teaching.

The Lord bless you and keep you,
Sheila

Prayers of Lament

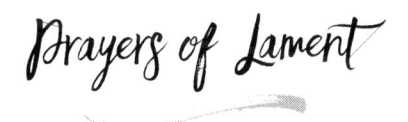

Fear and Worry

Change of Leadership
Change is difficult, Lord. We have a new leader, and my mind is racing in the face of uncertainty.

God, I pray your blessings on her tenure here. She will surely face resistance, whether in preserving routine or introducing change. She will have supporters, both genuine and self-serving. Give her wisdom, tenacity, and grace to navigate her new paths.

There are those who will remain devoted to our former leadership, even in her absence. Expand our capacity for hospitality. Help us recognize that welcoming one leader is not a betrayal of another as long as we share a common commitment to the well-being of our students.

Guide my heart through this season.
Amen.

Long Absence
God, you know the challenges I face when I am out of my classroom, even for a day. Help me manage the many days ahead. I do not know when I will return again or under what circumstances. Dwell where I cannot.
Amen.

ANGRY PARENT

Hide me in your shelter, Lord.
Where else can I go?
A storm of anger
gathered strength
and landed on me.
Unpredictable in force,
speed, or endurance,
it is upon me now.
Calm the fury
of the parent's heart.

Open my eyes
to the fear and love
that fuels the bluster.
Show me what I should do.
I am not always right;
humble me so I can apologize.
I am not always wrong;
humble me so I can forgive.
Amen.

I AM MOVING

Lord, you brought me to this place, I know full well. Your hand was in my interview and my acceptance of the position. You were present in my classroom and through these hallways. Now, you've made a path to a new position, and I will go.

I have learned and grown here. I have made dear friends and learned from mentors. Even my enemies have sharpened my skills and taught me how to live and forgive with grace. They are all woven into the fabric of my career.

As my departure grows near, the memories of first days, hard days, failures, and celebrations replay in my mind. The faces of students and their parents come to me. I recall the best of this chapter, though now it is bittersweet.

I think of work I am leaving undone. I am relieved of its weight yet burdened by the loss of opportunity. Investments of time and learning about this school will no longer serve me. I've built relationships that now will change.

I pack my belongings, and my heart's work is reduced to files and moving boxes. I wonder about the world in which I will unpack them. I will no longer be known. In a new place, I will not be given the benefit of the doubt. If anything, I will encounter only doubt.

Fear invades my thoughts. I am haunted by the comfort of my past, even if it is imaginary, a product of memory and hindsight. I question my decision, retracing the steps that led me here. I look for signs that I am on the right path.

Give me boldness to step into the next chapter of my life. May I carry with me the lessons I have learned and the wisdom I have gained in this position. Allow me to shed the weight of regret, even as I recognize that my grief is evidence of substance and significance. Nothing is meaningless. Thank you for your guiding light.

Amen.

BUDGET CUTS

Lord, there is apprehension in the very air we breathe. Once again, there is not enough money. It seems there never is.

An administrator has shown us the numbers and displayed the graphs, and we knew what they meant before she ever said it. We have seen these before, so we understand well that some among us will lose employment due to budget constraints. Meetings will take place. Spreadsheets will be projected and passed around while names of positions and salaries highlighted to determine who is "nonessential."

While they have their meetings, Lord, I come to you.

Be present in in the boardrooms as people make difficult decisions. May they realize the weight of their task and the impact it will have on individuals, families, and communities. *In your mercy, Lord, give them wisdom.*

Be with the campus level administrators who must be the bearers of devastating news. Give them grace and gentleness in clear, direct language. *In your mercy, Lord, give them courage.*

Walk with those who receive notice. Stay with them in their anger, sadness, and fear. Place opportunities in their path and give them eyes to see your provision. May peace rather than bitterness reign in their hearts. *In your mercy, Lord, give them hope.*

Be with those who surround the grieving. May they sit in silence without offering suggestions. May they listen, rather than speak. *In your mercy, Lord, give them compassion.*

Be with those who will remain on campus. Positions are being cut, but workloads are not. Help them figure out how to continue their work while covering the extra duties of those who are gone. *In your mercy, Lord, give them strength.*

Anger and Frustration

Animosity toward a Colleague

Help, Lord.
There is an enemy in my midst
that cannot be avoided.
Not only must I encounter her,
but I am forced to depend on her
to accomplish my goals.
How can I continue
with one who grieves me?

Her conceited and divisive ways
destroy morale and impede our
    work.
I am worn down by the effort of
    peacemaking,
and confrontation seems fruitless.
I only want to do my job,
but I cannot do it wholeheartedly
while her arrogance abides.
I cannot sleep for thinking of her.

I hear her mocking tone
and replay conversations,
rehearsing words I wish I'd said.

Lord, you are holy and pure of
    heart.
I will praise you for your steadfast
    love.
*Your mercies are new every
    morning!*[10]
Destroy the spirit that steals
    my joy
and renders me inept.
Heal the wounds sustained in
    battle.
The wickedness I hate in others
is the same I find in myself.
Have mercy on us, oh Lord.
Amen.

When Lies Are Told about Me
O God,

My enemies spread lies for power and pride.
Online, on the phone, in the Little League bleachers,
they spread their words of gossip and slander.

Lord, you know my heart, my intentions, and my actions.
How long will you let them go on?
They threaten my reputation,
but I am helpless to stop them or defend myself.
If you do not intervene, I will be ruined,
crushed by the burden of their dishonesty.

You are the God of justice and sovereign over all,
yet you endured lies and spoke words of love.
You were struck and turned your cheek.
I call out for justice;
Lord, teach me to be merciful.
Amen.

When a Child is Abused or Neglected
God of justice,
Make your sovereignty known.
Surely you hear the cries from the children who need you!

When will your anger rise against the ones who perpetrate abuse?
They are weak and cowardly
yet try to appear strong by attacking a child.
I despise them and their cruelty.

Children cannot wait for a system
bogged down by bureaucracy.
Bring your swift justice, Lord.
Strike down the ones who have inflicted harm.
Make yourself known to them so that they recognize the face
    of real power,
then leave them to tremble, cower, and beg for mercy.

Surely you will not hide yourself while we cry out to you.
I have proclaimed your faithfulness to the people
and told them of your righteousness and compassion.

You are the God who brings down the mighty
and has compassion for the humble.
You were there with David when he brought down Goliath.
As the bully hurled his taunts, you made sure the stone met its mark.
You removed the demons from the Canaanite girl
when her mother had nowhere else to turn.
You rebuked grown men
and invited children to come to you.

You who are slow to anger,
rise up now.
Amen.

Difficult Class

This class is a threat to my sanity.
Their behavior is out of control, and I cannot reign them in.
My attempts to build relationships have fallen flat.
They do not care for my encouragement
and refuse all my attempts at instruction.

My classroom is overtaken by chaos and apathy.
I watch the clock, dreading the time when they'll enter,
then yearning for the moment when they'll leave.
Surely, a year is too long to endure.
These students will destroy me much sooner.

In their presence, I doubt my abilities
and my very choice to teach.
In my suffering, I am at my worst:
incompetent, seething, and miserable.
How can they bring me so low?

They are your image bearers,
but I confess,
I cannot recognize your likeness.
Restore my sight;
let me see them as you do.
In you all things were created,
and *in you all things hold together.*[11]
Let your fullness dwell in me.
Hold us together in this place,
throughout this year.
Search me and know my heart.[12]
Reveal to me the otherness
that fuels my fear and leads to disconnection.

Heal my adversarial spirit
and renew my heart for teaching.
Recall to me my love
for my students,
then align my identity to my practice
so that I can enter this space
wholehearted.
Amen.

READY TO QUIT (1)

Every year, every day, I am asked to implement a new program.

Every year, every day, my students are more difficult to manage.

Every year, every day, the parents' anger increases.

Every year, every day, I receive less support.

Every year, every day, I am asked to do more.

I cannot carry on for another year, another day.

Every year, every day, you walk beside me, Lord.

I will praise you for your constant care all the days of my life.
Amen.

READY TO QUIT (2)
The demands are too many; I am ready to quit.
How will I explain to those around me
what I can hardly accept myself?
It is no longer desire that keeps me here,
but the shameful fear of leaving.
Must I admit defeat to those who always doubted,
or confess falsehood to those who believed in me?
Will I be humiliated among my coworkers and friends,
and will my enemies mock me behind my back?
If I stay, what will become of me?
But if I go, what will I do?

Lord, you call me blessed, and I know that I am.
From the deepest pit, you hear my pleas.
Deliver me from my despair!
Show me the way out of my misery.
Send me your spirit to guide my path,
so I can maintain integrity
as I transition from ruin
to new life.
Amen.

Poor Evaluation

I am brought low by my evaluation.
In a brief window of time,
a snapshot of my day,
I was judged to be
below the standard.
What truth can a brief visit reveal
to a tourist?
I am humiliated,
and in the wake of shame
looms anger.
In this state,
I cannot see
what is accurate
or what may be inflated.
You are the mighty God
and Lord of my life.
You enter my classroom
every day.
You know my strengths
and know where I am weak.

Turn my shame to humility
so that I can learn.
Replace my anger with reflection
so that I may grow.
Reveal whatever truth may be
in the words and the scores.
Teach me when to question
and when to keep silent.
Amen.

Frustration with my Low Position

How quickly those in positions of power have forgotten their beginnings. They strut through the halls, making quick judgments and shaking their heads. They make recommendations as though they know more about my students' needs than I do. They write programs and implement plans in attempts to dummy-proof the system, but why do they assume I am a dummy?

The newspaper prints what sells, and that is only bad news—the failing schools, unqualified teachers, and the qualified ones who expect reasonable compensation. Their headlines intend to make us the antagonists in our local drama, and the community buys it. They hop from public to private to charter school, following the trends, leaving behind a trail of teachers they've used up and worn down.

Television shows portray my profession as neurotic, having no standards or qualifications, rejects of other fields, turning to teaching as a back-up plan. Their depictions feed the myth that we are mere babysitters, overpaid for how little work we do. How much time do producers think we have for lunch, anyway?

Parents on a steady diet of pop culture speak to me as though I am a child myself. Some disguise their criticisms, but only slightly: "I know you haven't been doing this long" or "Maybe you've been doing this too long." Some yell and curse with no shame or recognition in the irony inherent in their behavior. "How are you fit to teach?" they ask.

Our positions are not likely to improve while we are allowed to make so few decisions for ourselves. Business executives and politicians write legislation that affects millions of children, but rarely the ones who dine at their tables. At state and federal levels, teachers are only invited to speak when it makes a nice photo op: #weloveourteachers.

I will trust in you, Lord. You will show me the path toward justice and teach me to love mercy. You promised that the first would be last and the last would be first. You are patient in suffering, but I know you hear my cries. In the kingdom of heaven, power will be overturned. Your strength is not a weapon but a fortress, a safe place where all may seek life. I will put my hope in the Lord, not in the ways of men. *Amen.*

Overwhelmed by Work

Savior, I call to you, though my voice is faint.

My to-do list is longer than today allows,
and tomorrow will be the same.
All tasks appear essential,
each one representing
another person's demands on my time.
I am crushed by the workload,
buried by expectations.

There is no relief in sight.
When the weekend arrives,
rest does not come;
there is too much to do
before the students return.
The burden is too great to bear.
I need a snow day, a sick day, a reason to stop.

I call on your name, strong deliverer.
You are the only one who can pull me out of this pit.
You are the God who gives victory.
You are the giver of life.
Raise me up, and I will give you glory;
renew my strength, so I can finish this race;
restore my spirit, and I will declare your ways! *Amen.*

Unjust System

Mighty God, you created a world in which every part works together. From the tilt of the earth to the cycles of air and water, your design was flawless. Human attempts cannot compare.

The systems governing the work of schools were flawed from the start. The original sin was in exclusivity, an effort to keep the downtrodden in their place. Attempts at reform have led to patchwork solutions that generate new problems. It is difficult to know whether such efforts are even legitimate or only hush money passed from the bothered to the bothersome.

And so, we have a school system in which the rich get richer and the poor get hand-me-down furniture, overcrowded classrooms, and a revolving door of teachers and administrators brought in to earn their chops or be driven out. Teachers and parents work on opposite sides of a chasm, neither one with enough clout to affect comprehensive change. Decisions are met with miles of red tape, and policies are made at least seven degrees from any child. Tests claiming to ensure equity and accountability become the tools for public shaming. Pay gaps persist, and no one can decide whether teachers are overpaid or underpaid, because no one is sure what they do with those "three months off."

God of the universe, reorder our system. I am mired in the absurdity of these structures. Remind me of my work and my reasons for doing it. May my individual path mirror the wholeness I desire at large. Let me live out my values and find like-minded community, then refine our focus and expand our influence.

Come to our schools, Lord Jesus.
Amen.

INEFFECTIVE LEADER

God, we all have so much to do.
My students crave my love,
their work needs my attention,
their families demand my time,
and the curriculum occupies my mind.
There are many things that I must do.

And Lord, there are things I cannot do.
Decisions above my status,
visions to cast,
actions to take,
and difficult conversations to engage.
These are not my job.

A leader has been appointed to the tasks,
but they are left undone.
We are weary and frustrated.
Anger flares, and hopelessness sets in
as I see my work diminished
by incompetence.

Clear the path for our administrator.
Remove the barriers that render her ineffective.
Give her the vision to lead us,
the clarity to prioritize her work,
and the courage to act.

Lord, guard my heart.
Grant me the self-control
to stay in my lane
and out of the way
as you do your work in her.
Amen.

Disregard for My Health

In a system built on power over,
who will listen to the voices
echoing down the hallways of our schools?
Where will my help come from?
I will raise up my voice.
I will speak the truth of our days.

We have been abandoned and betrayed
by the ones who claim to have our backs.
With one breath they hang banners in our honor,
and with the next they send us to play
a game of chance with our wellness.
They keep a safe distance,
behind our bodies, their titles,
and layers of red tape.

They set their guidelines but do not uphold them.
They make promises and forget
that such things require funding.
Do they consider us so insignificant,
expendable and replaceable?
When tensions rise and decisions must be made,
they are deaf to the cries from the classrooms.
We are here, and we know the realities,
yet rarely do they ask
what we believe is right or good.
Instead we are told,
and to respond with anything
but compliance
is considered lazy,
uncaring, and uncommitted.

We want to be with our students
and do our jobs,
but must it cost us our lives
and endanger the ones we love?
We are cast as villains,
while the enemy lives on
in the air we breathe.

My hope comes from you, Lord.
They are deaf to our cries,
but will you hear us?
Turn to us and consider our pleas.
We need protections
and the funding to keep them in place.
Draw boundaries around our spaces and our health.
Hear me, Lord, and I will give you the glory!
Preserve my life, and I will serve you!
Amen.

My Salary

Critics say that I should be satisfied. They believe that my work hours are a mirror of the children's school day and point to my summer off, not recognizing that I must take on a summer job. Why must I defend myself in the presence of so many who judge but do not know?

The public should defend itself to me! From the beginning they justified my low wages, not to reflect the workload, but because the salary was intended to support a single woman or to supplement her husband's pay. Times have changed, but attitudes have not. I am highly qualified and do my job well. The hours I spend in my classroom, in meetings, and working at home overshadow the monthly deposit into my account. I have bills to pay and a family who depends on me to provide.

You are a God of abundance. Lord, I will trust you to provide. Be present in my budgeting, saving, and spending each month. Make a way where there seems to be no way. I will declare your sovereignty in all matters of my life.
Amen.

Bored by the Work

Every day is much like the one before. I do my work, but I feel no joy. It doesn't excite me the way it used to. My feet shuffle from the car to the classroom as energy drains from my body. The days are busy, but they are not interesting.

I am restless. My mind wanders. The clock moves slowly, and I count the hours and minutes until I can leave. I check my email, reach for my phone, and hope for connection to a person or place outside of here. I am more energized as I leave the building than I am at any point while I am in it.

God, I confess my teaching is hollow. My students are fine, but they deserve more than mediocrity. Guilt is a heavy burden and not sufficient to lift the fog of my boredom.

Only your spirit can speak into my listlessness. Give me visions of a better way, whether in teaching or elsewhere. Grant me wisdom and courage to leave when it is time.

Show me the way I should go.
Amen.

GRIEF AND SADNESS

My Beloved Colleague Is Leaving
Lord,

You gave me a friend in this place. When my class made me laugh, I saved the story for her, because no one else would understand why it was funny. When stress threatened to overtake me, I went to her, and the burden was lighter when we carried it together. When I woke up too sick to teach, she knew where to find all of my sub materials.

Now, she is leaving this place. Who will I turn to in victory and defeat? I will be without a friend, even among my colleagues. To them, I am a name and grade level assignment to pass in the hallway with a quick hello. They do not know why I laugh or what brings me to tears.

Be my hope, oh Lord. Stay beside me all my days. You know my joy and my sorrow, for you created me. Before I speak a word, you know my thoughts. Therefore, I will trust in you. Even as I long for my friend, I will put my heart in your hands.
Amen.

My Beloved Principal Is Leaving

The Lord has blessed me with upright leadership. I've enjoyed a relationship of mutual respect. My principal knows that I will work with diligence, and I trust that she will lead with integrity. Now she is leaving. Surely, everything good will depart with her! Why, oh Lord, am I allowed to be abandoned?

The sea is roiling, and I can't find solid footing in the season of uncertainty. My status will surely change. The new leader will know nothing of my work or the reputation I've built. Campus priorities will shift as new pet projects take precedence over systems we've worked to establish. Shared philosophies and institutional culture will crumble. I will become an exile in my own land.

You are the God who has led me before and will surely lead me now. You will place new authority ahead of me. Then you will show me what I should do, whether I stay or leave. I will put my hope the Lord. Wherever you lead me, I will go. In change and in constancy, you will be by my side.

Amen.

LONELINESS

I feel as though I am all alone. Surrounded by people all day, there is not one whose ways are like mine. As I look around, I only see strangers, and I begin to question whether I am the one who is strange. How can it be that in a building full of people who share my profession, no one shares my heart?

In school and in experience, I have discerned what I value. I know how I should spend my time and what is not worthwhile. Such discretion seems offensive to my colleagues. I am simply too much for them. Or maybe not enough.

There is nowhere to turn and no one to turn to. Our struggles are not the same. When I speak, their faces stare without comprehension. I have learned to keep silent. I eat alone, even when I am among them.

I have stopped asking questions, because the things I ask sound like nonsense to their ears. Even in victory, I am alone, for they do not celebrate the things I count as gain. They mock me with their hollow voices and rolling eyes. They do not grasp the things that give me joy.

Lord, I am alone in this place. I withdraw into my own space, and in doing so, I shrink my very self. Over time, perhaps I will disappear and become a replica of the many who surround me. It will diminish my life and leave me going through the motions of imitation.

Lord, come and meet me here. Only you can save me from this life of hiding and isolation. In your presence, I am fully known, for you made me. You will strengthen me and raise me up to live. Even as I shrink among well-known strangers, you do not forsake me. Your presence comforts me and calls out to my true identity. I will trust in you all of my days.
Amen.

Missing My Children

I am energized and gratified in my vocation. I know that I am at my best self when I am engaged in the work of teaching. I can provide for my family and serve your kingdom by serving my students.

And yet my job demands sacrifice. I long for my family. I have missed my children's milestones while leading other children to theirs.

I weep when I consider all that I've missed. Each day they grow a little more; each year they become new people. Will I recognize them by the time we have another day together? Will they know my voice? Will they still reach for me when I return? I have missed so many firsts, and the question haunts me: if I miss the first, will the thousands after it mean as much?

Lord, you are good, and you have given me good work to do. I will trust you with my children. They are more precious to you than even to me, for you *knit them together*[13] and *know each hair on their heads.*[14] There is nowhere they can go that is not in your presence. Such knowledge is my comfort and my strength. I will not be afraid.
Amen.

Shelter in Place Drills

We have scheduled this time to teach our children how to hide behind locked doors,
to protect themselves from a person intent on killing.
It should not be so.

A calm voice will announce that we should shelter in place;
we'll remain until we hear the all clear.
It should not be so.
Our schools are full of children, and they should be safe places,
but we've seen how easily
they become a killing field.
It should not be so.

Where is your protection, Lord? When teachers lay their lives down, and families are changed forever,
when children cry out and their blood spills anyway, do you not hear their pleas?
It should not be so.

You promise resurrection and victory over death. Even as we sit in the dark,
huddled under desks and behind cabinets,
we proclaim that you are the Lord of life.
Lord, may it be so.
Amen.

Confession

I Lost My Temper

Lord, forgive me. I am the lowest of your servants. You entrusted these children to my care, and I have betrayed that trust. In my frustration, I spoke harshly. I unleashed my fears and failures on the students in my class. I gave in to the voices that tell me they should pay, should suffer as I am suffering. For surely, didn't they trigger my distress?

Yet, I feel the guilt that I know comes from the Lord. The Spirit stirs within me, shining light on the darkest places of my soul. My sin hides behind self-righteousness and false justifications, resisting discovery. Yet the Spirit searches it out and reveals it for what it is. I am low among all creatures, for I have sought self-satisfaction at the expense of a child.

The Holy Spirit convicts me, and I cannot stand. Have mercy on your servant, Lord. Do not depart from me or leave me in my shame. Forgive me. Renew my heart; I give it over to you.
Amen.

Circumstances out of My Control

I come to you, Lord, confessing my love of control. I have made it an idol, my strength and my salvation. I manage the class, structure the lessons, and set the pace. These are the skills that bring me success.

Now I am faced with circumstances beyond my control, and I see clearly how much I loved it. The grief I feel as I face my powerlessness leads me to anger and bargaining in turn.

God, I know you have lessons for me in this season. Hold me in the tension of strength and vulnerability so that I can submit to your ways. Teach me to loosen my grip and trust in things everlasting.
Amen.

Comparison (1)

I worked hard to make my classroom beautiful and inviting, and it was,
until I saw hers.
I created lessons that would engage and inspire, and they did,
until I saw hers.
I built relationships with my students so that my classroom would be a community, and it was, *until I saw theirs.*

Lord, have mercy.
Amen.

Comparison (2)

Carrying nothing more than a purse, other teachers walk out on the heels of the students. I am here into the night and through the weekends. This work consumes my days and my nights, my very life. And still, my classroom is a mess, I am behind on my grading, and so many of my students struggle. Why does it look effortless for others?

The energy is gone from me. My room and my lessons are all commonplace. And so am I. There is nothing unique or noteworthy in what I've done. I drag my feet through these ordinary days. I invited the enemy into my heart, and it has stolen my joy.

Lord, you are my refuge and my strength. Teach me your ways. Show me how to be inspired without coveting, to admire the work of others without allowing comparison a home in my heart. Better to please the Lord than my followers. Better one "good and faithful servant" than a thousand likes.

The Lord is my Shepherd. I will not want.[15]
Amen.

Self-Doubt

My students look at me knowingly. They have had good teachers before, and they recognize that I am not one of them. It is why they do not respond in the ways I expect or desire. Parents lodge their complaints, and perhaps they are right. Surely I am doing this all wrong, or it wouldn't be so hard!

My lessons are well-intentioned, but they fall short. I plan and prepare, but it seems no use. I still have disruptions in the classroom and low benchmark scores. Perhaps I am not suited for this work. The results I see are not equal to the effort I invest.

How long will it be before my coworkers notice my incompetence? Their offers of help sound like mockery in disguise. Do they speak of my failures in the office and the workroom? I want to hide in my humiliation.

God, save me from my own self-doubt. Replace my shame with reflection. Give me courage to recognize the ways I can grow and the energy to take meaningful action. Instead of hiding away, lead me humbly into community. *Amen.*

When Work Becomes Toil

I began this work with enthusiasm
and certainty of calling.
I earned my credentials
and was grateful to be hired.

Then the enemy came to prowl,
to steal, and to destroy.
Blessing turned to curse
and enthusiasm to dread.
Vocation has become
meaningless toil.

Every morning I wake up
more exhausted than before.
I greet my family in haste
before rushing out the door.
By the end of the day,
I have little left to offer.
My energy is spent;
my patience is gone.
They have things to tell me,
but my head still echoes
with the noise of the classroom.
They want to show and share,
but I've been watchful all day.

I need to be alone and to rest,
but there is no margin for respite.
In my weariness, I am unkind.
I put them off with assurances
that there will be time later.
It is the lie I tell myself, too.

I am wretched, Lord,
captive to my job.
It follows me home,
and I invite it in.
It consumes my days
and troubles my sleep.
I cling to competing
   commitments.
Choosing the trap
of "It's my job,"
"They need me,"
and "I only need to get through
   this"
over the freedom of Sabbath you
   offer.
Praise be to the Holy God
who delivered his people from
   bondage.
Hear my cries!
Release me from these chains,
   or I will surely die.
Reorder the priorities that I
   have thrown askew.
Restore my life to its fullness,
and I will praise you all my days!
Amen.

WHEN WORK BECOMES MY IDENTITY

God, you created me for work. You gave me gifts and revealed the ways I could use them. I do my job well: students thrive in my care; parents trust me with their children and seek out my expertise; I am honored among my peers for the value I provide. In my pride, I work with my whole heart, no longer for you, Lord, but for their praise. Work has turned to striving, and I am consumed by the hustle for approval.

Slowing down is unthinkable, for if I linger in stillness, what will I find? My home, my community, and my spirit have been left to rot and ruin. I have neglected once-nurtured corners of my life so that they are unknown to me now. Beyond work, I do not know my value. Beyond my job, I do not know who I am.

God, you made me, and you know me. Stay beside me as I face the shadows of my soul. Shine your light so I can see who I am, beyond the work that I do. Remind me of the gifts you placed in my being, and let me be satisfied to use them in service of your kingdom. Remove my hunger for earthly praise and restore my heart to your calling.
Amen.

Breath Prayers

INTRODUCTION TO
Breath Prayers

Dear Teacher,

I remember feeling in my first year of teaching that it was *always* 7:45 a.m. The students were *always* coming in to begin another day! No matter how late I stayed or how early I started, I couldn't figure out when I was supposed to get everything finished. I was always amazed at how much I could accomplish on workdays when the students weren't on campus.

Thessalonians says to pray without ceasing.[16] It's hard to imagine how we might spend a day in prayer when we have so many other things to do. Perhaps it would be possible to pray without ceasing if we could only find the time to get away from the noise and the work.

Living a contemplative, monkish life may sound appealing, but it is not the life of a teacher. It is good and important to carve out time for stillness and prayer, but for most of us, most of the time, that is not reality. Without the benefit of uninterrupted time, how can you pray without ceasing?

It may help to consider another thing you must do without ceasing. You breathe. You inhale. You exhale. Breath prayers, sometimes called centering prayers, are an ancient meditative practice. As the name suggests, they are meant to reorient us, to ground us in the here and now with the confidence that someone else dwells here, too.

The practice of breath prayers is simple. On the inhale, say (out loud or in your mind) the first four syllables. On the exhale, say the last four syllables. As you do this, follow the lead of your body. When you inhale, your body fills up with the oxygen it needs. On the exhale, your body automatically pushes out the gasses that would poison it. Your body has no malice toward carbon dioxide. It only recognizes it as toxic and so expels it. Likewise, your body does not give up in exasperation when, in the very next breath, more toxicity enters. Your body was made to repeat this process hundreds of times every hour.

In the same way, as you say a breath prayer, fill your mind with God's goodness in the moment, then empty your mind of anything toxic. There is no need to be frustrated or dismayed when toxic thoughts reenter your mind. Simply take in what is good, let go of what is not, and repeat the process throughout your days.

The prayers in this section are written for particular moments. Moments are fleeting, so these prayers may also be. It might be helpful to choose one or two of the prayers in this section to memorize, perhaps the ones you would use most often. Over time you can add to the collection of prayers that you can recall in a moment of need. My hope is that, as Kathleen Norris wrote, you'll find that "that such simple prayers, uttered at odd moments during the day, are an integral part of my process of conversion. And having to ask God for help also reminds me that I need the help of other people, as no one makes this journey alone."[17]

The Lord bless you and keep you,
Sheila

Breath Prayers

ON MY DRIVE TO SCHOOL
Inhale: For this new day
Exhale: I will be glad.

WHEN I'M LATE TO SCHOOL
Inhale: Keep me safe, Lord.
Exhale: Still my worry.

WHEN I STEP INTO MY CLASSROOM
Inhale: Your Spirit come,
Exhale: your will be done.

DURING BREAKFAST IN THE CLASSROOM
Inhale: Bless our breakfast
Exhale: and our bodies.

DURING ANNOUNCEMENTS
Inhale: Focus my thoughts,
Exhale: on gratitude.

FOR LEADING A CLASS DOWN THE HALL
Inhale: In every step,
Exhale: we walk with you.

Before a Lesson
Inhale: Give me wisdom
Exhale: and let me teach.

While Grading
Inhale: Focus and care
Exhale: until the last.

While Lesson Planning
Inhale: Show me the path,
Exhale: to teach and learn.

During Standardized Testing
Inhale: Let them slow down
Exhale: and remember.

During Standardized Testing (2)
Inhale: Our value is
Exhale: more than a score.

Before Checking My Email
Inhale: Make your light shine
Exhale: and give us peace.

Before Responding to an Email
Inhale: May my reply
Exhale: glorify you.

For Looking at Student Data
Inhale: Show me the truth
Exhale: and what to do.

When a Student has a Breakthrough
Inhale: Thank you, God, for
Exhale: shining a light.

When a Student Is Disruptive
Inhale: Show me her need.
Exhale: Give me a way.

When a Class Is Disruptive
Inhale: Give me insight
Exhale: and calm this storm.

When a Student Shows Compassion
Inhale: Bless the sweet times
Exhale: of tenderness.

When a Student Is Unkind
Inhale: Teach us the way
Exhale: to walk with love.

While Students Work Independently
Inhale: For all their growth,
Exhale: I am thankful.

When I Get a New Student
Inhale: Bless this student.
Exhale: Prepare her way.

When I Get a New Student (2)
Inhale: Love in my heart.
Exhale: Space in our room.

For Waiting at the Restroom
(with eyes lighting on each student individually)
Inhale: Bless ____,
Exhale: image bearer.

In a Moment of Silence
Inhale: Dwell in this space,
Exhale: dwell here in me.

When I Don't Feel Well
Inhale: Lord, I need you.
Exhale: Carry me now.

When I Need to Go to the Restroom but Can't
Inhale: I have a need.
Exhale: Provide a way.

When a Child Vomits
Inhale: Comfort ____.
Exhale: Give us clear air.

When I Want to Quit
Inhale: You are with me.
Exhale: I can remain.

When Passing the Cafeteria
Inhale: Bless those who eat.
Exhale: Bless those who watch.

During a Fire Drill
Inhale: Altogether,
Exhale: all staying calm.

UNSTICKING ZIPPERS AND TYING SHOES
Inhale: In all our needs,
Exhale: we think of you.

A READ ALOUD
Inhale: Bless our stories.
Exhale: Bless this reading.

DRINKING COFFEE
Inhale: God is my strength
Exhale: and my refuge.

HAND WASHING
Inhale: Lord, give us health
Exhale: and grant us life.

INTERRUPTED BY THE INTERCOM
Inhale: In this moment,
Exhale: I will be still.

FOR DISMISSAL
Inhale: Watch over us
Exhale: while we're apart.

DURING BUS DUTY
Inhale: In all the noise,
Exhale: you hear my voice.

WAITING FOR STUDENTS TO BE PICKED UP
Inhale: Bless and keep us
Exhale: until the end.

FOR A PARENT CONFERENCE
Inhale: Your image in me.
Exhale: Your image in them.

IN A FACULTY MEETING
Inhale: Unify us
Exhale: to do good work.

FOR TUTORING
Inhale: Bless our efforts.
Exhale: Make them worthwhile.

WHILE I CLEAN MY CLASSROOM
Inhale: Out of chaos
Exhale: you bring order.

WHEN I LEAVE THE BUILDING
Inhale: Leaving my work,
Exhale: lead me to rest.

ON MY DRIVE HOME
Inhale: Make me new, Lord.
Exhale: Renew my heart.

WAVES OF FEELING

(anger)
Inhale: In my anger,
Exhale: fill me with grace.

(frustration)
Inhale: Spirit of calm,
Exhale: voice of kindness.

(overwhelm)
Inhale: In the chaos,
Exhale: you are my peace.

(pride)
Inhale: Glory to God
Exhale: for my success.

(sorrow)
Inhale: In my sorrow,
Exhale: you comfort me.

(tenderness)
Inhale: Heart full of love,
Exhale: running over.

(weariness)
Inhale: I am weary.
Exhale: Lord give me rest.

(insult)
Inhale: Quiet my tongue;
Exhale: justice is yours.

Postscript

I am so grateful for the teachers in my life—the ones whose classes I attended, the ones I worked beside, and the ones I helped train. I have a growing appreciation for my children's teachers, who have taught remotely, virtually, and in the midst of uncertainty. I am grateful for the next generation of teachers, who will continue to shape the profession and prepare students for a world we haven't yet imagined.

I am especially grateful for you, reader. Thank you for inviting these prayers into your days, both extraordinary and mundane.

I am humbled and honored.

A Benediction

May the light of God
shine on your classroom,
may the love of Christ
flow from your heart,
and may the wisdom of the spirit
direct your path
this year and forever more.
Amen.

Notes

Introduction to Liturgies for Common Work

[1] "much of this labor is invisible": Ashworth, A. (2002). *Real Love for Real Life: The Art and Work of Caring.* Waterbrook Press.

[2] "in worship as in human love": Norris, K. (1998). *The Quotidian Mysteries: Laundry, Liturgy and "Women's Work."* Paulis Press.

Introduction to Prayers for Entering the Classroom

[3] "we teach who we are": Palmer, P. (2007). *The Courage to Teach: Exploring the Inner Landscape of a Teacher's Life* (2nd ed.). Jossey Bass.

Introduction to Prayers for the Community

[4] "we are one body with many parts": I Corinthians 12:12–17. New International Version.

[5] "have been taught to cope": Palmer, P. (1981). *The Company of Strangers: Christians and the Renewal of America's Public Life.* The Crossroad Publishing Company.

[6] in Christ all things hold together": Colossians 1:17, 20. New International Version.

Introduction to Prayers of Lament

[7] "full solar spirituality": Taylor, B. B. (2014). *Learning to Walk in the Dark.* Harper One.

8   "How can I be substantial": Jung, C. (1955). *Modern Man in Search of a Soul*. Harcourt Brace.

9   "a vocabulary to express": Pemberton, G. (2012). *Hurting with God: Learning to Lament with the Psalms*. Abilene Christian University Press.

Prayers of Lament

10   "Your mercies are new every morning!": Lamentations 3:22–23 New International Version.

11   "all things hold together": Colossians 1:17, 20 New International Version.

12   "search me and know my heart": Psalm 139:23, New International Version.

13   "knit them together": Psalm 139:13, New International Version.

14   "know each hair on their heads": Luke 12:7, New International Version.

15   "The Lord is my Shepherd, I will not want": Psalm 23:1. English Standard Version, paraphrased.

Introduction to Breath Prayers

16   "pray without ceasing": I Thessalonians 5:17. New International Version.

17   "that such simple prayers": Norris, K. (1998). *The Quotidian Mysteries: Laundry, Liturgy and "Women's Work"*. Paulis Press.

About the Author

Sheila Quinn Delony is a teacher, writer, and life coach in Franklin, Tennessee. She has twenty years of experience working with public schools and teacher preparation programs, and earned a Master's degree in Language and Literacy Education and a Ph.D. in Curriculum and Instruction from Texas Tech University. She has published academic articles in the field of education, as well as short stories relating her grandma's childhood stories. She enjoys gardening, hiking, and reading good books with her husband and two children.

As a life coach, Sheila works with ambitious women who possess integrity and good humor. Her clients have a habit of accomplishing the things they set out to do, but they may experience frustration or dissatisfaction because their roles and ambitions overlap in challenging ways. Through the process of coaching, they learn to bring their values and priorities into alignment so that they can experience both freedom and fulfillment in each area of their lives.

Sheila's spiritual retreats are designed to explore prayer through creativity and imagination. They draw from both liturgical and extemporaneous traditions and include both communal and individual prayer practices. Participants engage in guided and self-directed journaling and mediation, as well as tactile exploration of prayer through the arts.

If you are interested in individual coaching or a group retreat with Sheila, visit **sheilaquinn.com** for more information or email her at sheilaquinnresources@gmail.com. You can also follow her on Instagram @sheilaquinndelony. To sign up for her newsletter and bonus content, including downloads of many of the prayers in this book, visit sheilaquinn.com.

About the Artist

A twenty-year independent musician, Eric Peters has released eleven studio albums. In addition to music, Eric is a visual artist, piddler, and bibliomaniac. He lives in east Nashville, Tennessee, with his bride, Danielle, and their two sons. Eric's music and visual artwork can be purchased at **www.ericpeters.net**.

Made in the USA
Columbia, SC
24 March 2025